The Anatomy of Survival

The Anatomy of Survival

STEPS ON A PERSONAL JOURNEY
TOWARDS HEALING

Una Kroll

CONTINUUM
London and New York

Mowbray
A Continuum imprint
The Tower Building
11 York Road
London SE1 7NX

First published 2001

Unless otherwise stated, scriptural quotations are from the New Revised Standard Version © 1989, 1995 Division of Christian Education of the National Churches of Christ in the United States of America

British Library Cataloguing-in-Publication Data
A catalogue record for this book is available from the British Library.

ISBN 0-264-67530-4

Typeset by BookEns Ltd, Royston, Herts
Printed and bound in Great Britain by
TJ International Ltd, Padstow, Cornwall

Contents

Acknowledgements

In preparing this personal account of some of my steps in the journey from a series of disasters towards healing through the experience of survival and growth, I am grateful to the many people in my life who have helped me along the way. Some, like my parents and my Aunt Nellie, are now dead but their influence on my life has been, and continues to be, profound. Others are still alive. Many of these people, friends, former patients and parishioners, have helped me by their example. They have struggled to survive disasters that most of us will never have to encounter. Others, especially my friends, have encouraged me to look for healing even in desperate situations. A few people have tried to push my head under the water, so to speak, and to these I am especially grateful, for, had they not done that, I should never have known that I did not want to drown. I wanted to survive. I wanted to do more than that. I wanted to live and to grow and to find healing. By the grace of God I have done so, and now I want to share what I have learnt with those who are struggling to find meaning in their own lives and to do more than literally survive.

In the text I have put certain case studies in italic type. These studies are taken from life, but special effort has been made to conceal the identities of the people involved. The portraits are therefore composite ones. Accounts derived from my own life and that of my husband are factually true as far as I am aware.

I am grateful to the Revd Elaine Dando and Miss Betty Houghton for their helpful advice on parts of this book, which I asked them to read.

I offer special thanks to my present spiritual director, Fr Donald Allchin, and to Fr Keith Dennerley, Sr Marie Greene RSCJ and Sr Maraid Quigley RSCJ, all of whom have accompanied me, from time to time, during my personal struggle to learn how to grow through grace.

Acknowledgements are due to the Division of Christian Education of the National Council of the Churches of Christ in the USA for permission to quote copyright material in the form of Biblical quotations.

In memory of Sarah, who died
and for
Robin, who survived

Introduction

'Without victory there is no survival.'
(W. S. Churchill, 13 May 1940)

I was fourteen years old when I read those stirring words of Winston Spencer Churchill in a speech made to the House of Commons during the Second World War. It was delivered barely eleven days before the beginning of the evacuation of the British Expeditionary Force from Dunkirk to the shores of Great Britain. The words, that sounded so grand and poetic at the time of the speech, made me expect an imminent victory which, of course, did not happen. Some four weeks later our newspapers were full of descriptions about the flotilla of small ships that had rescued 335,000 Allied soldiers from the beaches of France, to which they had retreated in the face of the oncoming German army.

It is possible, depending on who you were, and where you were, at the time of the British Expeditionary Forces' retreat from France in the months of May and June 1940, to see the evacuation of Dunkirk as a disaster or as a victory. Perhaps it was both. It was a disaster for the people who were killed, maimed or captured, and those whose lives were permanently changed by the death or disappearance of their beloved relatives. It was a victory for those who survived and for the people who brought them home over the English Channel.

Churchill's words continued to puzzle, even to plague, the mind of the girl who saw some of the soldiers immediately after their return to England. I can still remember agonizing over their exact meaning. Where was there victory in defeat? What did survival mean? Was his statement true? Was there a way in which mere physical survival could turn into more than mere physical victory?

The endless questions in a fourteen-year-old girl's mind were not answered at the time, but subsequent encounters with various kinds of disaster have given me insight into the meaning of disaster, survival and victory. This book is the fruit of that experience.

Disaster can be a difficult word to define because its precise meaning depends on the degree of distress or disruption caused to an individual or group of people by a calamitous event or emotion. In this book I have defined disaster as any event or emotion that seriously disrupts the rhythm of people's daily lives.

The simplest definition of survival states its meaning in purely physical terms. To survive is to live on after some life-threatening event, after personal disaster that changes one's life for ever, or after the death of other people. I can describe myself as a survivor in all those ways. When I was a young girl, my mother reached a point of despair: she tried to kill us both, but neither of us died. We survived. In the Second World War, I lived on when many of my generation, including members of my family, were killed. Life was not the same as it had been before the war. I have outlived my parents, my husband and many friends of my own generation.

I do not, however, want to measure survival in such a narrow way. If I were to do that, I would have to state that continuing to be alive is the only measure of victory over actual or potential disaster, and I do not believe that. Experience tells me that there is more to survival than simply continuing to be alive on earth after the physical death of another, the awful emotional trauma of the death of a marriage, the permanent loss of health, or the humiliation of being unable to work, whatever the reason.

The quality of continuing life after physical or other kinds of death is important to survivors: that is why Churchill's words, which at first I did not really understand, ultimately became important to me, for they introduced me to the notion of survival being linked to victory. Victory implies an overcoming of death or disaster: it adds a dimension to survival that I both appreciate and try to find in my own life. I also look for victory in the lives of others whom I meet.

In this book I have approached the subject of survival mainly through personal experience. It is comparatively easy to talk about disasters, survival and victory in rather vague terms, or even in learned theological discourses which obscure the overwhelming impact of disaster on an individual's life. Sometimes such an approach can dilute the reality of disaster and the awfulness of physical survival in the absence of any sense of real victory. It is partly for this reason that I have chosen to describe the anatomy of survival in my own life, but there is also another reason.

When I was a medical student we dissected a human body to learn its anatomy. We knew that other human bodies were similar in structure and organ anatomy to that one body. We also knew that not all bodies are absolutely alike. There are variations and these are important, particularly for those who would become surgeons. In general, though, the study of that particular body helped us to recognize the likeness of one to all. Similarly, I believe that the anatomy of survival has a shape and structure that is common to all human experience, and that, although there are variations, all of us can learn much from the experiences of one person. That is the second reason that has prompted me to use myself as a prime source of study. I will, however, be discussing some experiences that are not personal but which I have seen from outside, so to speak, because the richness of human experience cannot be fully compassed by one person's adventures.

There is another dimension to this book that needs to be made explicit from the outset. The Christian religion is part of my own humanity. It has formed me and shaped me and I cannot separate my humanity from my faith. As a Christian I believe that physical death is not the worst thing that can happen to a person. Christ's victory came after a real death. He did not survive. He entered resurrection life. So it is not life as it was before death that I am looking for when I meet survivors of terrible disasters. It is resurrection life, new life, a life that has its proper connections with the person's previous life, but also has an altogether new quality that was not there before. Death, physical or emotional, is the gateway to that new life. The new life, enabling a fresh start to be made, is a gift that is available to those who have died *and* to those who have survived disaster in which there has been death: the death of a beloved person, the severance of a precious relationship, the termination of a former way of life that accompanies financial disaster or forced redundancy.

In introducing into this book the concept of resurrection life, life after death, new life that springs from the old but is altogether different, I am aware of the dangers I face in trying to communicate with those who do not share my faith. Christianity is burdened with concepts and words, even at times with jargon. Some words have a special meaning to insiders but not necessarily to outsiders. I hope to show that resurrection life, in the sense that I am using the term, transcends concepts and words that define one faith or one kind of human experience over and against another. It is an experience that is common to our humanity irrespective of our religion. If that notion is strange to you, please do not judge its truth until you have reached the end of this book.

1

The shape of disaster

'Out of the depths I cry to you, O Lord.'
(Psalm 130:1)

My life has been one of adventure from beginning to end. It has been a good life, on the whole a happy one, but from time to time it has been beset by disaster.

In this chapter I shall be looking at the shape of disaster as I reflect on the past years of my life. Disaster, as I have already said, is an overwhelming experience. While I admit that what appears to be a calamity in one individual's life can seem to be only a hiccup in another person's history, I have selected only those unfortunate events in my own life that have seriously threatened my physical existence, my health and my mental balance. Survivors cannot afford to be over-emotional about their negative experiences nor can they easily make fresh starts after disasters if they get lost in self-pity. The fact of disaster is so real that it needs to be approached practically. With hindsight I can approach some of my past misfortunes with a certain amount of humour. At the time, survival was my only goal.

The first real disaster of my life came through the experience of being born. I was unaware of this at the time, but the course of my life was, nevertheless, profoundly affected by the circumstances surrounding my conception and birth.

My parents were born and brought up in Russia in Tsarist times. My mother was born in 1893 and my father in 1895. They knew each other as children, but as adolescents their lives diverged. My father married his first wife when they were young. I think they already had conceived a child by the time that he and my mother were thrown closer together by their work as underground intelligence agents in Russia. Both worked for the British government during the First

World War. My father was an active spy, my mother his courier. Both were supporters of the Tsarist regime of that time.

I am told that it was during this period of their lives that they began to fall in love, despite my father's status as a married man. I am not surprised. Life in those days was cheap. Love was a way of fending off thoughts about imminent danger and the possibility of death. When you are working closely with someone in conditions of extreme danger, moral issues are not uppermost in your mind. If my parents did fall in love they did nothing very definite about it, as far as I know, and they certainly never considered my father's divorce to be a possibility at that time.

By 1918 they were in serious danger of arrest and my father arranged for my mother to escape to England by plane. He, himself, simply took off his disguises. He dressed up in his best British Army uniform and walked on to a railway platform just as the British ambassador to Russia and his party were leaving the country. The communists recognized him, of course, but they did not want to precipitate a diplomatic incident so they let him get on to the train and leave their country.

After their arrival in England my father returned to his wife. My mother began to travel 'to get over him'. She worked in Istanbul doing 'something in intelligence' and then went off to India to help my father's sister, Marguerite, have her first and only child. In the spring of 1925 she returned to England via Rome where, fortune would have it, my father happened to be on a visit. He was still married and, by this time, he had two children.

So, I was conceived out of wedlock. I was certainly not wanted, and in today's climate I might have perished before birth, but the mores of the time was against abortion. Illegitimate birth would have stigmatized my mother and myself in the class-ridden society of the middle 1920s. The solution, thought up by my aunt, my mother and some of their friends lay through the purchase of a divorce for my father, the money being supplied by one of my aunt's rich friends. This was duly accomplished and by the time I was born they were wed.

My father's former wife, and my two half-sisters, were left without much financial or emotional support. Later on, my mother and I were to find ourselves in the same state. My father was not a bad man at all; he just did not understand marital responsibility. He was highly responsible in his professional life but never managed family responsibilities or money well.

I was unwanted, certainly, but much loved by my mother after I arrived. Had I been a son I might have been loved by my father as well, but he already had two daughters and, tragically for us, he was already in love with a woman who was to become his third wife, so really the marriage was doomed from the start.

He left when I was about eighteen months old. I do not remember his going, though my mother told me that I cried for him for several weeks. I do, however, remember my mother and I 'going home' to her own mother when I was about three years old. By this time our only means of subsistence was my mother's sewing work in a basement sweatshop, staffed by Russian exiles. So we went the cheapest possible way. Our destination was a small village called Libau in Latvia.

My very first memory is of my mother playing card patience games during a long train ride while I sat perched up on the table by her side with my nose pressed against the carriage window to look at the pine trees by the side of the railway tracks. I can remember the sound of the wheels, the early morning flame-coloured sun, the unmarked snow on the ground stretching from track to forest, the trees extending into the distance as far as the eye could see. As I looked, I sensed a feeling that the happiness of those moments was all mixed up with sadness. The sadness came from my mother's soundless weeping as her hands dealt the cards endlessly for hours on end.

That is all that I can remember of that particular journey but on every other journey it was the same, except that never again were there such tears, and never again was I small enough to sit up on the table, having to sit instead on the seat, squashed up between my mother and the window. Later memories tell me that the huddle in the third-class railway carriages in Europe generated some warmth, which was a good thing, as it was remarkably cold. Each time we went to Latvia we travelled that way, until, on the last occasion, when I was twelve years old, my mother earned enough money to indulge in the comparative luxury of the covered seats of the second-class carriages. During each journey the snoring in the compartment at night would be periodically interrupted by passport, ticket and customs officers at the borders of each country. With mutterings and groans, and not a few oaths, the slumbering adults would search through layers of clothes to find their documents, hand them over for brief scrutiny and then resume their noisy chorus as soon as the sliding door was closed. When dawn came we would move stiffly, and, in turn, made our way to the smelly lavatory down the corridor, where we would try to wash our faces and hands relatively clean from the accumulated grime of the journey. Food would be unwrapped from rather grubby red, green and grey handkerchiefs, and shared around. This was an event I enjoyed. People talked excitedly to each other in many different languages, and I, often the only child in the carriage compartment, would often pick up choice titbits and sweets when my mother was feeling indulgent, or was not looking too closely at what was going on.

My second conscious memory also comes from that very first visit to my grandmother's home in Libau on the Baltic coast. We climbed up the rickety steps to the covered veranda, and stood shivering before the only door into the house. It was Christmas time. Snow covered the ground and icicles hung from the sloping gutters. There was a huge, or so it seemed to me, wreath of holly and ivy on the door leading into the living room. It was awesome. I had never before seen anything like it. The door opened wide into warmth and laughter.

This was to be our first positive experience of life after the sad death of a marriage. For the warmth behind that wooden door transformed our lives, at least temporarily. My mother was laughing, laughing, laughing for the first time; it must have been for a long time or I should not have remembered it. The samovar, the big Russian tea urn that was part of our family life, was on. I, drooping with tiredness on arrival, was put to bed in my Aunt Nellie's big bed in a small room just off the main living-room. It had no door. I lay there sleepily awake, listening to a happily reunited family as they wrapped my mother into their love. I must have fallen asleep, for when I woke in the morning the very ample body of Aunt Nellie, my mother's older sister, lay beside me and, at our feet, under the blankets and between the sheets, lay her two cats. That was where they always slept, and that was how I always slept on our visits until I was over five years old.

In describing the anatomy of my first conscious experience of disaster, the break-up of a marriage that had been contracted for the wrong reason, I realize that my response to that event also set a pattern for survival which was to stand me in good stead in later life. As a very young child, I learnt to sit very still and hold other people's sadness inside myself without being able to do anything about it except gaze out of a window into a different kind of happiness. Whenever I did this, I found that, after a while, the sadness simply dissolved into the happiness. In later years that was to become almost a way of life for me, certainly a way of being with, and praying for, unhappy people. It has often been as if the other person's sadness was infectious and I caught it – rather like catching chickenpox – but, in a strange way, if the sadness disappeared into my own happiness, then my happiness could also be caught. If happiness is too strong a word for what happens, and I think it often is, then something of my own peace and stillness in 'looking out of the window' can sometimes be shared with other people, particularly those who are sad. The ability to communicate that is pure gift. It certainly comes from that very early experience, and I would say it has been a major part of my own work as a medical doctor and Christian healer.

My next significant personal experience of disaster came when I was five years old and circumstances forced a separation from my mother who was, I think, ill at the time. She could not look after me properly. As a temporary measure she entrusted me to the family of a friend. I was to be a companion to a girl three years older than myself, in Riga, Latvia. My Aunt Marguerite accompanied me to the ship. Just before she left, she told me that if ever I were so unhappy that I wanted to come home, I should let my mother know by drawing her a picture of a ship. If I did that, my mother would know that I was desperate.

I had no premonition whatsoever of the homesickness or unhappiness to come. Some of the subsequent misery came to me because I had the misfortune to be brighter than most children of my own age and certainly brighter than my older companion. Since, at our joint lessons, I 'showed her up', she became jealous and the inevitable happened.

Masha, though that is not her real name, was larger, taller and stronger than me. We shared our bedroom. As soon as the lights were turned out we were supposed to be quiet and go to sleep. Masha was angelic until that moment, but as soon as the room was dark she would start tormenting me, either by whispering terrifying tales or by climbing stealthily out of bed to come over to mine and pinch my arms and legs or do anything else that would make me cry. That was the whole point of the exercise.

I had no way of fighting back. I was small, lonely, frightened. I cried for help, but none came. Instead my companion's angry father would appear at the door to find out what all the noise was about. Invariably, it was Masha who told him, but it was never the truth. Inevitably, her tale brought me the punishment, always introduced with those scandalous words which grown-ups use to children: 'I'll give you something to cry about.' At first it was only a good spanking on my bare bottom. Later, it was a strap.

I do not think I was badly hurt in my body. In my adult years I have worked with many children who have had far worse treatment than was meted out to me. I am certain that I was not indecently assaulted within the technical meaning of that word. The man would not have thought of himself as a child molester. In his opinion I deserved what I got and the various refinements of pain were administered to make me understand the iniquity of upsetting someone who, out of the kindness of his heart, had taken me in as a companion to his daughter. Yet, these night-time episodes were to have a lasting effect upon me. They caused me to associate the genital areas of my body with pain. They caused me to be frightened of sexually aroused males. They caused me to feel that I deserved to be punished. They caused me to despise myself for succumbing to tears. And, worst of all, they caused me to become confused, because at one stage, when I felt that I could bear no more pain, I found a way of escaping it by going back in my mind to my Aunty Nellie's big bed where I had once known real love. So, somehow, the pain and the love all got mixed up and pain became a way of reaching ecstasy. This too was to have serious repercussions in my adult years.

In my misery and fearful anticipation of almost nightly pain, I remembered what Aunt Marguerite had told me about drawing a ship and sending it to my mother if I was really unhappy. I was. I sent my picture to my mother. No reply came. Much later on in my life, I found out that my aunt had forgotten to tell my mother about the code we had arranged. Week after week, I would wait for the letter that would deliver me from my total misery. Week after week, nothing came. Worse still, sometimes bland cheerful letters would arrive saying how wonderful it was that my kind 'uncle' and 'aunt' were taking care of me. These letters always ended by telling me to be a good and grateful girl.

Eventually, a full year after I had left England, I returned home. The separation from my mother, and the physical and emotional abuse, had left me with scars, but none of them equalled the damage done by the searing disappointment at being 'let down' by an adult whom I had trusted and upon whom I had relied.

I had survived but there was no victory. I was not the same child as I had been when I had left England. I was a disturbed child who was angry with my mother for abandoning me when I thought I had so plainly appealed to her for rescue. I took it out on everyone, but especially on the two relatives whom I most blamed for my misery, my mother and my aunt. I remember behaving in an abominable fashion, testing their patience to the limit with my constant whining demands, grumbles and negative reactions to simple requests from them. There were no child psychiatrists around to advise the unfortunate adults who were trying to help this fractious child. I think they shared the burden, turn and turn about. Neither knew, then or later, that because of what had happened to me in Riga I would be afraid of all male adults. It would take many years of living before any glimmer of victory would come out of that year of profound unhappiness. Yet, come it did, because of the love and sensitivity of one man, my husband.

Life went on. The last episode in my early childhood that affected my adult life came at a time of extreme poverty and misery in London some time in 1931.

Towards the end of that year, life must have become extremely difficult for my mother. I remember the day when she came home knowing that there was no more sewing work to be done. The next day she did not go to work as usual. Some time after that, there came a weekend when she and I had nothing to eat in the house except for one egg and some Bovril. That was all there was. She gave me the choice. I chose the Bovril. She ate the egg. We crawled into bed to keep warm. My mother and I always slept together, a habit she kept up until I was fourteen years old; more, I think, through our joint need for warmth than through emotional need.

It may have been that weekend that she tried to kill herself and me, or it may have been a little later. All I can remember is being tucked up in our big bed facing the window on to the street. To my left, on the side of the room nearest to my mother's side of the bed, was a coin-operated gas fire which was seldom lit because we had no money. The coins my mother managed to save up were always left on top of the meter and were used when the weather was really cold. On that particular evening there were quite a few there. It was a windy night. My mother told me it was cold and said she would stuff up all the cracks in the windows and doors so that we could turn the fire on and get warm. I lay in bed and watched her going round the room lining the windows with our old jumpers and skirts and coats, stopping up the crack under the door on my side of the bed. My ears were cold. I snuggled down under the bedclothes to get them warm, waited sleepily for the fire's glow and fell asleep.

In the morning I woke with a splitting headache. There was a ghastly smell in the room. My mother was still asleep beside me, her arm under my head. It was very cold. I wanted to go to the toilet. I got up, staggered across to the door and opened it. When I came back my mother was awake. Her headache was equally terrible. I climbed back into bed and she cuddled me fiercely, then began to cry. We clung to each other and stayed in bed the whole day. There were no more coins on the top of the meter and there was no food in the house.

'I must have left the gas on,' my mother said, 'and the wind blew the fire out.'

I did not really believe her then and I do not now. One of her best friends in the sweatshop had killed herself only a few weeks before. My mother's attitude towards that tragedy had been philosophical. She regarded it as a blissful end to unmerited suffering. In later years my mother would laugh and say that our lives were saved because she had insufficient money to put into the gas fire meter; a laugh which, by that time, was genuine enough in its thankfulness.

Whatever the truth was about that weekend, it had a lasting effect on both our lives. Immediately afterwards, my mother wrote to my father and went to my Aunt Marguerite for help. My father sent a large chicken. I can remember it arriving before Christmas. That, he said, was all he could afford. I can still remember my mother's scorn when she read the note that came with the parcel. She never approached him for help again, but we enjoyed the chicken and lived on it for over a week. My aunt gave more practical help. In 1932 my mother found work again as a secretary to a hair shampoo manufacturer, who needed someone who could speak foreign languages. We were never again to be as poor as we had been during the last half of 1931, though we came close to it at the end of the 1939–45 war.

My mother's pride came to our aid. Finding herself alive, whether or not she wanted to be, she seems to have determined that I should grow up into a person who would be free from the kind of misery she had experienced. From that time on, she decided that the only way a woman could avoid helpless dependence on either non-existent men or non-existent money supplies was through education. She knew I was intelligent and she was not going to let me fail to acquire a good education if she could help it. She would work, and so would I. I might need battering into conformity, and at times I did, but she never deviated from her purpose for me. All her energies were bent to this task. She earned what she could, begged what she could not earn and forced me to my books in every possible way. Her private life virtually disappeared, since everything was subordinated to this single aim. My social life was almost non-existent, since I was always at my lessons or homework. Apart from some wonderful holidays with my Aunt Marguerite and my cousin, and our summer trips to Libau, which became more infrequent from this time onwards, I knew no respite from the round of school, homework, adult company and sleep.

At an intellectual level, I responded to my mother's strategies for my education. I loved her. I needed to please her. At a psychological level, however, I was more adversely affected by what had happened to us during that winter. It coloured my attitude towards money, and that attitude persisted. As an adolescent and young adult I became quite unable to cope with any thought of running out of food or money. If there was food available I would eat it, hungrily, greedily, storing up against the time when there would be no food. I grew podgy and then obese; at times of emotional crisis I still overeat compulsively. At times of stability and happiness I have no such need and can control my appetite quite easily. This attitude towards food and money was to be a handicap for many years, and it lingers still in my emotional responses. I am getting much better than I used to be, but it has taken many years of patient awareness of my conditioning to help me to overcome the emotional consequences of my early experiences of poverty.

It must not be thought that I was an unhappy child. I was not. During my formative years there were nights of bliss in the home of my mother's Hampstead friends, when I would listen to her laughter rippling round the supper table, know that she was happy again and bend my mind in turn to my own pursuit of pleasure. There was plenty of that to be found in books, in some school homework, in writing stories and in drawing pictures. Lost in a world of my own creating, I needed little outside company, and it was during those years that I learnt how to enjoy being alone. That ability to be alone without being in the least bit lonely has been invaluable to me in my adult years. It was during those years, too, that I taught myself how to get things I did not want to do done quickly, so that I could get on with the things I did want to do. My ability to concentrate and to work quickly was formed during those early school years when I wanted to get through boring homework as soon as possible in order to make the good use of the hours before bedtime to draw or write stories. I saved reading for bedtime, when, once I was in bed, no one ever came up to turn off the light and tell me to go to sleep. They were too busy downstairs around the always-boiling samovar, telling each other stories about pre-revolutionary Russia.

During those years I also developed an ability to speak several languages and, at the same time, to cut myself off from anything that might distract me from focusing on what was of immediate interest to me. I lived in the middle of a cosmopolitan multilingual commune. I grew up fluent in English, Russian and French. Everyone in our friends' household, which was a kind of second home to my mother and myself, spoke several languages, often changing languages many times during one conversation. This babble of languages was constant, and I quickly learnt to pay attention only to what concerned me directly, or what interested me, in the adult conversations that were always going on in my presence. I have enjoyed being a polyglot, even though I have forgotten much of my Russian since the death of my mother and aunt. I have profited even more from my ability to listen selectively or to abstract myself totally in the middle of a crowd of people.

The disasters of the years before I was six shaped my later responses to other times of difficulty. The disaster of my birth, my father's early departure from our home and a later knowledge of the disadvantage of being a girl, left me with a sense of guilt at having been born at all. The experience of separation from my mother and of subsequent physical and emotional abuse caused my innocence and trust in authority figures to die. Our extreme poverty and my mother's attempted suicide left me emotionally handicapped. Yet, each disaster contained its own mechanism for survival and I have been unable to resist the need in me to describe the seeds of that survival along with the description of the shape of disaster.

By the age of six I had discovered that I wanted to be alive, that I could go on living even though part of me had died, that I could live with handicap. I had already found it possible to experience pain and happiness simultaneously. I had discovered a way of finding happiness in solitude. I had also found that all forms of self-pity and recrimination are a waste of time and energy. Sterile ruminations about why awful things happened and how they might have been avoided, simply hindered one from being able to tackle the pain and to enjoy what could be enjoyed. Nothing was going to stop me from looking for happiness, and nothing did.

There is one later episode of my childhood that was to affect my whole life. When I was eleven years old I met my father again for one day. We met at his sister's home in East Sussex. We spent the day together and, in the late afternoon, drove home to London on the old A23 road, stopping off at a roadside cafe for tea where there were some white Angora rabbits for me to see and hold as we talked. The conversation on my side had been stilted throughout the day, but I had a secret plan inside my head and was determined to put it into action. I was going to ask this stranger to come back and look after my mother and be my father. Now, I thought, holding a beautiful Angora rabbit in my arms, now is the time to ask him.

At this time of my life I knew little about my father, except that my aunt had told me that he was a very brave man who had won many decorations during the First World War. My mother had countered this picture with one of her own. She told me that he was a drunkard, a womanizer and an irresponsible father. She told me to look out for his charm. He had been charming that day. He had made me feel loved and cherished, and it had been a happy day in the company of my relatives. The pictures in my mind were confused. My heart longed to know this man better. Such is the innocence of a child hungry for a father, and I was innocent. I opened my mouth to speak and at that moment he spoke first.

My father cannot, of course, have known of my dreams and hopes. As far as he was concerned this was a 'getting to know each other' sort of an exercise. He asked me if I knew he had remarried? I did not. In that moment my whole being turned to ice. The Angora rabbit wriggled. For a brief space of time I buried my face in its fur. Then I put it down, got into the car with composure and remained silent until we reached home. I thanked my father politely for a lovely day, got out of the car and left without a backward glance.

After that meeting my father and I were not to meet again until I was eighteen years old. I think that some of my adolescent disillusionment about adults in general started that day. I had a hard time growing up into a young adult, trusting no one, least of all if they were male, and confiding in no one. But I also have to say that the kind of work I was to do as an adult was also determined that day, and for that I am grateful. I had nurtured an ardent desire to bring my mother and father together. I had failed to do so, but the internal need for them to be reconciled was still present. It was to have a profound effect on my personal life, on the way I worked as a doctor and, later, as a minister of religion.

Although I did not know it when I was eleven, I can now see that the sudden and forced realization of the difference between fantasy wish and impossible goal was, ultimately, helpful to me. What happened to me that day was to sow within me a determination to check out fantasy against reality, and that was to make it much easier for me in my adult life to accept situations where healing of a partnership was not possible, but healing of individuals through separation was. That insight has been helpful therapeutically to many people who are trying to break away from distorting relationships and are held back by intense guilt.

Happily, my own experience did not make me a cynic. While I could not reconcile my mother and father, and stopped trying to do so from that day onwards, I could unite the disparate elements in my own personality I had inherited from them. Scarcely knowing what I was doing at the time, I began to pursue that goal of integration, inadequately at first but, eventually, with considerable success. The capacity to do that has undoubtedly helped me in my work with adults in partnerships that have dissolved, and also in my work with their children, who often feel pain and guilt about their parents' separation.

The pattern of disaster had been established. All the subsequent calamities of my life have been measured against these earlier episodes. Nothing in my adult life comes close to these particular childhood experiences. It so happens that all of them were unavoidable, as so many disasters are. I did not choose the circumstances of my birth. I did not choose separation from my mother. I was not responsible for our poverty. I did not anticipate that my father would tell me bad news. Seen against the backdrop of major environmental disasters, such as earthquakes, hurricanes, tidal waves and tornadoes, these minor episodes in one person's childhood years are relatively trivial. Nevertheless, they are the episodes that form an unbreakable link between myself and other people, wherever they are in the world and whoever they may be. They have given me insight and compassion for those trapped in disasters that are not of their own making. They have precipitated prayer and concern for people who find themselves in desperate circumstances through events over which they have no personal control.

Some disasters, however – usually those that occur in adult life – are of our own making. These look like disasters to those who see them from outside, yet they may contain hidden blessings. In my own life, my marriage began as a disaster and ended as such a blessing.

2

Disasters that contain a hidden blessing

'Mine enemies speak evil of me.'
(Psalm 41:5a; AV)

Some disasters lead to unmitigated pain for those who survive them. The death of a child, for instance, may leave an indelible print on the lives of those who have to live on. Some find a way of living with their pain. Others may never come to terms with what has happened. Some are left with wounds that burst open from time to time.

In 1910, when my future husband Leo was eight years old, he and his seven-year-old brother, Adolph, were playing with a group of boys in a street in Honolulu. On Leo's prompting they suddenly decided to cross the road. Leo reached the other side safely. His brother was hit by an oncoming car. The bone of his fractured leg was sticking out through the skin. He was taken to hospital and seemed to be making a good recovery when tetanus set in and he died. Later in his life Leo wrote:

> I believe that my poor mother never recovered from the anguish of this; for the rest of her life she always had a small picture of Adolph with her. Although she and my father inevitably must have blamed me for this, I cannot recall them saying so, but the whole incident must have made a lasting scar on my subconscious and so have somehow affected my whole life.[1]

When he grew into an adult, Leo chose to go into the Order of the Holy Cross, a monastic order for men based in New York. Later he wrote: 'My conscious motives at the time were that I felt I needed more training for the priesthood, both intellectually and spiritually, but there may have been other deeper reasons for my coming to this decision.'[2]

Leo's father was a priest who, subsequently, became the Bishop of Liberia. I do not think that Leo becoming a priest and a monk was a simple matter of following in his father's footsteps. I suspect that he was prompted to do so by a sense of guilt about his brother's death, which he concealed even from himself for many years. By his own admission, he was temperamentally unsuited for a celibate life. It must not be thought that Leo's thirty years of monastic life were unhappy. They were not. He found great fulfilment in his fifteen years of work in Liberia, becoming, in turn, a responsible novice master, assistant Superior and finally Superior. It was only long after we were married that he could bring himself to talk about his brother's death and its full meaning in his life before we met.

Forty-seven years after Adolph's death, and with its consequences still operative but not obvious in his life, Leo met me in Liberia at a time when he was the Superior of the Order and I was a junior sister in the Community of the Holy Name. Our meeting was not propitious. It was the consequence of a crisis of my own making.

By this time in my life I had rebelled against my mother's desire that I should become a relatively affluent and respected member of society. She had chosen a medical career for me with my full compliance, but I had then decided to become an ardent Christian, which was not at all to her liking. I was clever and well positioned to become a successful member of the medical profession when, in 1953, I decided to throw ambition to the four winds and become a nun.

My choice was an unhappy one for my mother. It did not meet with approval from any of my elders in the medical profession either. I was a profound disappointment to them, since I was considered capable of 'rising to the top', and few women in those days had any chance of success in that way.

Stubborn as I was at the time, as well as an idealist, I became a nun and was professed in temporary vows on 14 September 1955. Members of my English community worked in Liberia in close association with American members of the Order of the Holy Cross, who had established a Christian village in Bolahun, a village in the hinterland of Liberia, in 1919. It was to there that I was sent in 1956 to replace an American doctor member of the Order who was on extended furlough. Having been relatively happy in my life in the community up to that point, I found myself struggling with an intense conflict between my duties at the Mission hospital and my duties as a junior nun at the convent. In my own mind, some parts of my work as a surgeon and doctor had to take precedence over my duties in the convent, but that attitude did not fit in easily with my way of life as a professed nun. Moreover, personal difficulties between myself and the American doctor on his return from furlough added to everyone's problems.

The conflict caused trouble, so much trouble that some influential members of the Mission wanted to send me home. Other people, including the majority of the Liberian villagers, wanted me to stay. Petitions were sent to America. As a result the Superior, my future husband, decided to come out to the Mission to settle the matter.

He arrived in February 1957 and spent the next two months listening to people of varying opinion. I did not make life easy for him. I did not want to go home and I fought to stay.

By this time I had established myself as a good surgeon. Unlike former Mission doctors, who were male, I was able to be with the village women during childbirth and allowed to operate on them if they could not deliver the child naturally. Several women had been delivered of healthy children through Caesarian section. Aware of the dangers to these women of trying to have more children in the absence of a doctor who could perform this life-saving operation, I had already written to my Reverend Mother in England asking her to give me adequate warning should she wish to recall me at any time. In that case I would offer these mothers sterilization, as they would die if they tried to undergo a normal labour with a cervix firmly closed by the disease of schistosomiasis that was rife in that area of the world.

My arguments were to no avail. After weeks of listening, Fr Kroll delivered his verdict to me in church; I meekly kneeling, he wearing dark glasses and sitting with a pet chimpanzee on his lap. The dark glasses concealed any feelings he might have had about what he was doing. The chimpanzee, was, I supposed, a kind of distraction from the awfulness of his message, namely that I was to be sent home as soon as possible.

It felt to me like a disaster, a decision that spelt a death-knell for many of the mothers and other patients who would not now be able to have the operations they so badly needed. On hearing the news I clenched my fists so hard that the nails bit into my flesh. I got up from my knees and departed to the convent.

I became ill, so ill that I could not return home for several weeks. When I finally recovered and left Liberia I was still far from well, and it was thought wise for Fr Kroll to accompany me as far as Paris. At that time my mother and his brother both lived in Paris. Our intention was that Fr Kroll would return to New York from there after a short visit. I would return to England after I had convalesced with my mother. By this time I knew that I would have to leave the Order to which I belonged, but I was still afraid of returning to a secular life.

When Leo and I parted company at Orly airport I did not expect to see him again. We had grown closer to each other during my illness. During the next few days I missed his companionship. I think that my mother knew I was in love, but I did not. When Leo rang, I accepted an invitation to go sightseeing. It was then that he disclosed to me the fact that my struggles had resonated with his doubts about his own vocation to remain a monk.

I listened. After several days of listening to his life story I knew that he could not continue with his penitential life as a monk. There were wounds in both of us which needed healing, and, looking back on that time from a distance of over forty years, I suppose we both instinctively knew that we had found something in each other that gave us hope of being healed. Within a few days we admitted that our affinity had started to turn into love. We found ourselves unable to part company. It was characteristic of both of us that our first action after this discovery was to go to Sacré Coeur, a famous church in the heart of Paris, and spend an hour in front of the Blessed Sacrament.

When two previously responsible members of the church make an uncharacteristic decision, it is as well to ask why. We could not answer that question at the time. We were both contrite about breaking our vows of religion. We did not seek to justify our actions. We were both deeply sorry that we were about to hurt so many of our former friends and members of our respective religious communities. Neither of us pretended that our love for each other absolved us from the sin of breaking our religious vows, but we also knew that we would not go back on our decision. So we began the difficult task of disclosing our intentions to get married. We returned to England and were taken in by kind friends in Birmingham. They did not approve of our intentions, but they did not withhold their hospitality.

From our Orders' point of view, our decision was a considerable shock. They could not perceive any reasons for our behaviour other than the obvious one of a breakdown in moral fibre. Senior members of both religious communities came to Birmingham from America and Worcestershire to do what they could to prevent us from taking such a terrible step. Of the two of us, Leo had the most to lose. He was in life vows. I was not. His monastic vocation and priesthood were at stake. I could obviously earn my living as a medical doctor. Perhaps it was inevitable that the senior people in both Orders, as well as senior clerics in the Episcopal Church in America and in the Church of England, should focus their attention on saving my husband from making a terrible mistake.

The opposition sealed our determination. It confirmed our love, even though we were not to discover its deepest blessings for many years. It also settled our punishment. We were married at Birmingham Registry office on 1 June 1957. On the same day, a letter came from the Bishop of New York suspending Leo from active priesthood. Seven weeks later, on 22 July 1957, Leo was deposed and formally expelled from the Order. The Order refused to dispense him from his vows. This decision was meant to call Leo to his senses and to help him see that he was guilty of grievous sin every day that he spent with me. To a man of his sensitive conscience it was a severe punishment.

Subsequently, Leo received a letter from the Archbishop of Canterbury saying that he would do his best to see that Leo would never work again in any Province under his jurisdiction. Leo never had paid work as a priest again. Out of compassion, and believing that the Order was wrong not to dispense him from his vows, Leo's bishop, Bishop Donegan of New York, formerly a good friend to Leo, and the Visitor to the Order of the Holy Cross, allowed him to act as a priest again after just over a year. Nineteen years later, the Order relented and dispensed Leo from his vows. The day the letter arrived, Leo opened it, read the contents and, for the first and only time in our thirty-year marriage, expressed his anger with the Order for the years of spiritual and mental suffering he had endured at their hands.

Such things would not generally happen now. There is a more compassionate mood around. Priests, even religious superiors, can leave and marry and remain priests. Nuns can leave their orders and remain friendly with their former sisters. I can, and do, thank God for these changes. They are in line with the church's gradually changing attitudes towards the remarriage of divorcees in church. It is punishment enough to have to live with the knowledge that one's marriage has failed, that one has broken vows of religion. I have not yet met any Christian who is light-hearted about the failure of their marriage and their inability to remain faithful to religious vows, but external punishment, continued for too long, can be very destructive to recovery of self-esteem and self-trust. Punitive retribution does not sit easily with ideas that it is possible to be forgiven by God.

Our marriage, according to conventional wisdom, should not have been successful. Leo was twenty-three years older than me. We came from different backgrounds, different cultures. Leo was in a strange country and he was unable to work as a priest, the only work for which he was fitted. He took a low-paid job with a missionary society. For my part, I scarcely knew my way around the National Health Service. I worked as a locum doctor until I was able to find a better job. We were, however, tougher than we or anyone else knew. The struggle to survive cemented our love for one another. Moreover, both of us believed that God had forgiven us and would help us to make a fresh start in our lives.

So we did just that. Our marriage did survive. Indeed, it flourished. During the next thirty years both of us grew into people we could not have become without the support and help of God and one another. Over a period of years, Leo gained insight into his guilt over Adolph's death and was able to enjoy the freedom that he had discovered through stopping his self-punitive penance in the monastic order. He thoroughly enjoyed fatherhood and our four children kept him young in heart. During those same thirty years I learnt to forgive my parents for the unhappiness of some of my childhood experiences and I grew into a contented person, one who knew she was loved by God and her family, even though she was despised by some of her own Christian community.

In a strange kind of a way, both of us were healed in a manner we would never have thought possible at the beginning of our marriage. My work with disadvantaged women in society and in the church became, for both of us, a means to restoring my self-confidence and self-respect. It was an indirect way of repairing some of the damage that had been done to me as a young girl. I also felt it was a positive way to make amends for the damage I and others had inflicted on some of the women whom I had abandoned when I left Liberia. So, yes, I am deeply thankful for my marriage, and for my healing that came from God through a beloved husband.

As for our two religious communities? No one is indispensable. They recovered from their loss. Indeed, both went on to renewed strength.

Looking back at this time in my life, I am aware that Leo's mistakes, notably as a youngster when he called his brother across a road, and my own, which led to my having to leave my work in Liberia, looked like unmitigated disasters. Certainly they were disasters, but they were not irredeemable, nor irremediable. Ultimately, Leo forgave himself for his brother's death. I too gained insight and a measure of freedom from some dangers inherent in my own personality. I am positively glad that I am someone who has broken vows. It has stopped me from ever feeling 'holier than thou' about other people. I have found it possible to get on with life without blaming anyone else for misfortunes that have come out of my own sins or errors of judgement. That is not to say that retributive punishment is necessarily just or beneficial. I can testify that it is not. Gentleness and mercy are far more effective forms of helping sinners to come to repentance. My own frailty has given me insights into the hidden reasons for other people's imperfections, vulnerabilities, sins and mistaken actions that I could never have gained had I remained a virtuous nun.

Perhaps the greatest gift that has come out of this episode in my life has been a growing ability to accept forgiveness from God, learning to forgive myself and to allow the past to slip into the past.[3]

It seems to me that most human beings will have encountered some disaster in their lives that is of their own making. After any such event, provided that they are honest with themselves, they may be able to admit their own share in its genesis. More importantly, they may be able to see why the event has happened. People often repeat mistakes they have made before, but those who take the opportunity to reflect on such mistakes may learn to understand themselves, to forgive themselves and to break the vicious circle of repetitive behaviour. Disasters, such as divorce, alienation in relationships, dismissal from work or errors of judgement, may provide us with opportunity for reflection, forgiveness and growth. They need not always have permanent embittering consequences. Instead, they may reveal hidden blessings we would never have known about had the crisis not occurred.

I do not in any way think of our marriage as a disaster, but I can see that it felt like one to other people whose lives were entangled with ours at the time when we both decided to get married. Those having pastoral care for people who make decisions that seem to be unwise or even idiotic need, I think, to listen very carefully to the life stories of the people in their care. If they do that, they may be able to find the hidden blessings that God can use to heal those people. Leo and I were singularly fortunate in finding each other. Both of us listened and went on listening until the tangled skeins of our lives could be unravelled by God. Few are so blessed.

Disasters, whether they be undeserved or deserved, do not always lead to an impulse towards survival. That is a sad fact of life. It is also a mystery as to why some people are able to survive and others lose their way. Perhaps it is possible to approach this mystery by looking in some detail at one of the worst disasters that can befall human beings on their journey through life; that of physical and emotional bereavement.

3

The disaster of bereavement

'[Jonah said], "It is better for me to die than to live".'
(Jonah 4:8b)

I have a lot of sympathy for Jonah. First of all he is asked by God to go
to Nineveh, a city of wickedness, and prophesy against it. Naturally,
he is appalled by the magnitude of the task and tries to escape. So he
boards a ship going in the opposite direction. When a terrible storm
rises, Jonah is seen to be the cause of God's displeasure and, at his own
request, he is hurled into the sea to appease God. God, however,
intends to see that Jonah will do what he is told. So God provides a
large fish to rescue him and then returns relentlessly to the request
that Jonah should go to Nineveh. This time Jonah obeys, even though
he secretly hopes that the people in that big city will not repent so that
God will punish them with disaster.

When the people of Nineveh do repent and God remits their
punishment, Jonah is furious; so furious that he asks God to let him
die rather than see the consequences of God's mercy. But he is not
allowed to die. He finds a shady bush and settles down to see what
will happen to the city. The cool of a bean plant gives him some
delight but, before long, God allows a worm to attack the bush. It dies
and Jonah is exposed to the elements, a hot sun and a fierce east wind.
Jonah is so angry with God for this second attack that he again asks
God to let him die. Instead, he is left alive and treated to a discourse
about mercy.

For a very long time I could not read that story with any sympathy
for God or the people of Nineveh! My heart, my emotions, were
wholly with Jonah. Life seemed pretty unfair. Like Jonah, I wanted to
escape suffering. Like him, I felt resentful when others escaped justice.
In one respect, however, I differed from Jonah. I was never able to

echo his words, 'It is better for me to die than to live', until I had to live on after the death of my husband. The deaths that preceded that death did not have quite the same effect.

Bereavement after physical death

During the Second World War, my mother and I found ourselves in London during a period of intense aerial bombardment. It is true that the sound of nearby anti-aircraft guns in Hyde Park was comforting but it did not diminish the fear that the next bomb to fall would be the one with our name on it. It did not take away the silent horror of seeing the ruins of nearby buildings when the air-raid was over. It did not mitigate sadness when two of our neighbours were killed. The fact that we had survived yet another night of heavy bombing was a source of thankfulness, but our grateful hearts were accompanied by a sense of guilt at still being alive when a mother and child three doors down the road were dead. Why, I asked myself, should they have been selected for death when I and my mother were left alive? There was, of course, no answer to this awkward question. The very randomness of sudden death had unnerved me.

As the war continued, young friends serving in the forces were also killed. The casualty lists grew. When I was about seventeen years old, I found myself thinking about my three cousins, all of whom were in the German Army. I had a premonition that all was not well with them. Indeed, it was not. Two of them were killed on the Russian front. The third was captured and spent twelve years in a Soviet gulag before being released. We did not hear that news until after the war, but there was still shock when the letter came.

Bad news of such magnitude, however it comes, etches itself upon one's memory. There are the immediate physical side effects. Much later in my life, I remember picking up the telephone one morning to be told that my mother's cancer had returned in force and that, 'there is nothing more we can do now'. My body felt drained of its blood. I felt very cold. My head spun. There was, I remember, no question of disbelief. I became aware that although the hospital doctor's work was finished, mine was only just begun. I had to find the strength to take care of my mother and help her to die. The immediate shock passes but the stark memory remains.

By the time my mother died I was over forty years old, a mature woman with a husband and four children. I had been a practising doctor for fourteen years and I was accustomed to imparting bad news and to caring for those who had to go on living. I was also used to bad news myself. During our marriage we had suffered reverses in fortune: at different times both of us had lost jobs and we had encountered real poverty. We had lost our first child through miscarriage. I had also faced all sorts of disappointments through being a woman rather than a man. It is true that my experiences were somewhat unusual – most people do not become missionary nuns and then leave to marry a missionary monk – but, if one looks closely, some kinds of traumatic events can be found in most people's lives. At the time of my mother's death, I still had a loving husband's support and four lively children to bring up. The shock and grief at the various disasters and bereavements in my own life were subsumed into the sheer necessity of getting on with the work in hand with the help of the loving support of a close-knit family.

When, however, twenty-two years later my husband died, it was different. The immediate effects of shock were still there – I can recall the moment of his death vividly – but life after his death was altogether different from that of life after my cousins' death, my miscarriage and my parents' deaths. This time, when the immediate shock passed, the funeral was over, our loving adult children had gone home and I had to return to work, I discovered that I definitely did not want to be a survivor. I did not want to go on living.

I suspect that suicidal ruminations among survivors of physical bereavement are more common than professional carers want to accept. The survivor may feel ashamed of such feelings and conceal them from everyone. Close relatives may suspect that suicide is a possible option but feel too embarrassed to raise the issue in discussion. In my own case, the pain of living was compounded by an innate tendency to depression, which had plagued me at times throughout my life even when things were going well for me. I had also been sensitized to the option of choosing to die through my own mother's attempted suicide and through the deaths of several of her Russian émigré friends who had found that suicide was preferable to their lives of abject poverty in exile. My own suicidal ruminations continued for an uncomfortably long time.

I have always respected those who, finding life intolerable for whatever reason, decide to die. Within the span of my own professional life as a medical doctor, attitudes to suicide have changed greatly. When I was young, it was treated as a crime, and people who unsuccessfully attempted suicide were often prosecuted and punished. Those who assisted suicides were also punished. Christians regarded suicide as abhorrent and those who managed their own deaths were refused Christian burial. By the time I became a young doctor in 1951, suicide was considered to be the product of a temporarily deranged mind. This was a compassionate attitude and it also provided Christians with a convenient way of enabling someone to have a dignified funeral. All the same, I found it quite a shock when, in 1988, I saw the Anglican Church's official change of attitude put into action. In that year, a notable Anglican priest, Dr Garry Bennett, committed suicide. His funeral was conducted by bishops and senior Anglican Church dignitaries with 'full ceremonial'. By the turn of the twentieth century, it was recognized that some people took their own lives for reasons that were comprehensible both to themselves and to others.

In some countries, euthanasia, or assisted suicide, is now legal if a patient is suffering from a terminal disease. A few years ago, a Dutch friend of mine, a priest, chose this way to end his life. I spoke with him on the telephone a few days before his death. He did not tell me of his intentions, but it was very clear that he was in his right state of mind, that he knew his life was coming to an end and that he wanted to spare himself and his immediate family any further suffering. His voice sounded so happy and strong on this occasion that I found myself quite shocked when I received the news of his death less than two days later. I cannot personally agree with this practice but I do at least begin to understand those who make this choice.

If, however, bereaved, and temporarily depressed people like myself choose to go on living they will seldom find that survival has any resemblance to the life they knew before death. In my own case, survival was a drab, dreary, wearisome business for well over two years. I woke each morning with dread, knowing that the day would feel like being in a desert land without sufficient water to last through until nightfall. I treated the beginning of each day with intellectual objectivity, establishing in my mind that I had sufficient intellectual reserves to continue to do my job reasonably well. At the time I was working with a child protection team and I knew that other members of the team would soon tell me if my standard of work fell below acceptable levels.

There is a sense in which I divided myself into two people. One was the automaton, the robot, who ate, talked, examined children, comforted parents, made careful medical assessments and went to court to give evidence on behalf of parents and children. The other was the 'controller' or 'overseer', the person who observed the robot dispassionately to assess its capacity for accurate work, and who, to some extent, protected the robot by establishing careful patterns, almost rituals, to cope with possible signs of incompetence.

Neither of these two people had any sentient emotions. Those were consigned to some subterranean space deep within me. Each day of the year after my husband's death, I worked hard – too hard. I had to go on working late into the night to avoid the moment when memories and feelings might return. Being a doctor, I knew that I might resort to drink or drugs, so I was careful to have access to neither. Being a well-informed person about the effects of bereavement, I knew that feelings of anger at being left alone, and feelings of guilt as to whether I could have done more to keep my husband alive or to help him more, were likely to surface. When they did, I regarded them with scientific detachment. Such a cold way of going about the business of living was well-nigh intolerable, yet emotional breakdown was impossible to countenance.

Since that experience, I have heard many bereaved people speaking with hindsight about their 'coping mechanisms' during the months and years after a partner's or child's death. Overdrive through hard work, staying up late watching television (without actually seeing or understanding what is going on), restless walking through a wakeful night, are just some of the common ways of dealing with unassuaged, recognized or unrecognized, grief, particularly when the survivor is living alone. Guilt at being alive at all, when the person one most loves is lying in his or her grave, may also lead to one focusing on good works to avoid the dread feelings of guilt and grief. One of my close friends, for instance, decided to put her inability to sleep to good use. She became a night-sitter for people who were very ill or dying. When morning came, she was exhausted enough to get some sleep during the day. On the other hand, I worked during each day as an automaton without feelings, because I did not want to feel any emotion at all. Emotions were dangerous. By midnight I was tired enough to fall asleep for a few hours. In the morning I would sometimes find myself in front of a television set that was still churning out its productions.

The flattening of my emotions had other side effects too. I became timid with my children, unable to speak about my feelings lest these should add to the grief they were experiencing in turn. They, I thought, were reacting as I had done when my mother had died. I did not want to add to their problems, but I had no reserves to draw on to offer them the help they so desperately needed. I worried about them all the time, but worry is not the best expression of love. It can be very irritating. I became mute with friends and had to keep the conversation at an impersonal superficial level so as to avoid emotional responses. I missed the company of my children and friends but was defensive if they approached too often or too closely. I was determined not to be a nuisance.

During the early stages of this bereavement I found it helpful to know what was likely to happen. Scientific observation by many different authorities over a period of years has established a pattern of 'normal' bereavement. Shock is succeeded by anger, then by depression and finally by adaptation to loss, which amounts to a willingness to make a fresh start in a new phase of one's life. All these stages overlap and last a variable length of time.

Shock

I did not suffer for a long time from shock. My husband's death was anticipated. Nevertheless, when it happened there was a short period of denial and disbelief. People who hear the news of an accident, or who lose youngsters on the seashore, or who experience the horror of the sudden murder of a relative or close friend, are subject to much greater trauma than those who have had time to get used to the idea. Those who suffer such awful disasters are sometimes blessed by a long period of numbness, or sometimes by feelings that the dead person is still present in the house or about to return alive and well. The truth that the person one loves is dead only dawns slowly. During that period, a widow or widower may suffer from repetitive disbelief. This is nature's way of dealing with shock. Usually, such a period of shock is over by the time of the funeral, which serves as a marker of the reality of death. Professional help is only needed if the denial of reality is unduly prolonged.

Anger

Once the immediate shock has passed, survivors often feel anger towards the people who have been involved in some way in the death of a person they love. This anger surges up whether the 'agent of death' be a murderer, a drunk driver, or a professional who missed a diagnosis or made an error during an operation. Anger may also be directed against professional carers who looked after the deceased during his or her terminal illness. Often this anger is misplaced, being directed against perfectly competent professional people. It is known that mourners are hypersensitive during the early stages of bereavement. Usually, patience and good pastoral care enable such anger to subside in time.

Sometimes, however, people's anger is justified. Relatives of the dead person may be justified in blaming incompetent or insensitive professionals such as doctors, nurses, social workers or priests for things that have gone wrong, or for injudicious remarks made during that person's illness. If incompetence can be proved, there is some sense of satisfaction in bringing the offender to justice.

Justifiable anger may be very difficult to handle, especially if it is made worse by poor professional responses to accusations made, or insensitive refusals to accept responsibility for things that went wrong through professional error. When incompetence is exposed, and some redress made, the process of ultimate recovery can be assisted. Sometimes, however, legal processes take so long that the beneficiaries are emotionally exhausted by the end of them.

During the early and intermediate stages of bereavement the survivor may find him or herself angry with the dead person for leaving them. The irrationality of such a stance makes no difference to the anger. It is there. It should be listened to and respected.

Anger with God is also common among survivors and can occur at any stage of grief. I have chosen to discuss this aspect of survival in more detail later in this chapter.

Depression

Depression in the medium- to long-term period after bereavement is usual, even when the immediate ruminations about suicide have subsided. Relatives and friends have to be patient when the survivor needs to rehearse the death again and again, needs to weep, needs to be consoled for seemingly long periods of time. Gradual recovery from depression is usual, yet the first signs of returning pleasure in life sometimes provoke guilt, so this phase of the grief process needs to be treated with some care.

Knowing that there is a typical pattern of behaviour for a survivor after the death of a spouse was helpful to me, but, like many other people in the same situation, I relied a bit too much on the pattern, expecting recovery before it was ready to come. Clinicians say that the re-establishment of satisfaction and pleasure in being alive should take place within about two years. All I can say is that many years of listening to survivors tells me that many people conceal the fact that they have not reached such a stage in two years. They feel guilty about it and hide it well. I certainly did. It took me four years to discover any real joy in life. I can still recall the disappointment and guilt I felt when the two years had passed and I was still living in what felt like an arid desert. Now, I warn bereaved people that there is no fixed time limit to any stage of recovery from grief. That warning diminishes guilt and anxiety when things do not go quite as expected. That is not to say that I think people have no need of help during the years of their aridity. They certainly do, but I do not rush to label them as 'abnormal' or, necessarily, prescribe medication if their grief seems prolonged. Any hint of that kind of attitude can sometimes result in their withdrawal into further concealment and silence. Each of us deserves to be treated as an individual and our needs are also individual.

BODILY DEPRESSION AND LOWERED RESISTANCE TO ILLNESS

The body's defences against illness are lowered by depression. It is known from scientific studies that morbidity and mortality are increased among survivors during the year following a severe bereavement. I was fortunate to find myself handicapped by increasing deafness, severe tinnitus and vertigo, which came on a few weeks after my husband's death. I say fortunate because I might have had a much more severe illness than any of those. The deafness interfered with my ability to hear the small children that I was working with each day. That, and the other symptoms, forced me to seek medical help, and eventually led to early retirement from my medical work. These handicaps were permanent, but medical help and adaptation of my way of life have ultimately enhanced my quality of life and my enjoyment of it.

I could as easily have had a heart attack, developed a gastric ulcer or cancer, or suffered a nervous breakdown. The whole person is affected by the task of survival after severe bereavement. Some people die prematurely. Others survive handicapped. Some ultimately adapt to a new way of life. What matters is that survivors and their close relatives and friends know that the year, or years, following a death are times when survivors are vulnerable to disease.

GUILT AS A MANIFESTATION OF DEPRESSION

Guilt is often a manifestation of depression. Many people find that, during the early period of life as survivors, they are plagued by feelings of guilt. Some feel guilty at being alive when those whom they love are dead. This can be particularly acute when someone has survived a serious accident in which another person has died. The same sense of guilt at being alive may afflict survivors of natural disasters like earthquakes and tornadoes. Amazement at finding oneself alive, coupled with 'why me?' feelings, can all but overcome people who have been released from hostage situations where others have been brutally killed. Two of my missionary friends, who had been tortured before being released from imprisonment, felt terrible grief at knowing they had escaped while others were still in captivity. They wanted to go back to the countries from which they had been expelled, even though they knew that to return would expose them to the risk of death. They also knew that they would subject their relatives and friends to further suffering. Their desire to return might seem selfish rather than heroic to outside observers, but that is how they felt.

Other people, like myself, do not feel guilty about being a survivor. They do, however, feel guilty about their conduct towards the dead person. All kinds of unpleasant memories surface. I have already written about the way in which some people blame professionals, but self-accusation is also common. A common experience is that of accusing oneself of neglecting early symptoms and signs of the disease that finally killed one's spouse or child. Doctors like myself often hear relatives of dead patients saying things like, 'I could have done more', 'I was so often impatient when he complained', 'It's awful, but in the end I wanted him to die'. If the surviving relative was also the prime carer, to whom the giving of pain-relieving medication was delegated by professionals, then he or she may even feel instrumental in killing the one who has died. Survivors need a great deal of help if they are to deal creatively with such natural feelings of guilt.

There is a tendency among survivors to conceal ruminations of guilt, in the same way that suicidal feelings are concealed. Professionals, such as doctors, nurses and attending clergy, need to take responsibility for uncovering and dealing with guilt before it takes too firm a hold. Simple reassurance does not always help. It may, indeed, make things worse. Religious people are not always comforted by rituals such as prayers, confession and absolution, especially if they are undertaken prematurely. Caring professionals have to be endlessly patient in their listening before a survivor can intuit the difference between true guilt and false guilt and so find freedom from both.

A further effect of being a survivor is the fact that there will be part of one's life that is shared with one's former partner and part of life that will never be shared. My husband died when only one of our children was married. Our son was married three weeks after his father's death. Our two daughters married within the next two years. None of our ten grandchildren were born before his death.

IMPAIRED JUDGEMENT IN THE DEPRESSIVE PHASE OF GRIEF

When people are depressed after a serious bereavement, their mood alters and their perceptions and judgements are often impaired.

I suspect that the judgement of individual members of our family was quite deeply affected by my husband's death. Our two children who had married before his death have remained in stable relationships. The other two, who married within two years of his death, have separated from their partners. Their grief after their father's death may not have affected their judgement in seeking their marriage partners, but I would not be surprised if it had.

I, myself, certainly made important decisions during a time when my judgement was severely impaired. After my husband's death I went on living in our joint home, but the October storms of 1987 precipitated a decision to move. My elderly and handicapped neighbour, and I, both living alone, were sited on a three-acre plot of land at the top of a quiet lane in a village in the south-east of England. On the night of the great storm, our telephone lines were torn down. The electricity was cut off for over a week and there was substantial damage to some of the trees in the garden. The fallen trees had only missed our homes by a metre. Subsequently, both of us decided to move. That decision, coming as it did only four months after Leo's death, was the right one for me, as subsequent events were to prove, but I made it while I was still bereaved and the move increased my sense of loneliness. It retarded healing.

My four children, loving towards me as they were, felt powerless to prevent me from selling up and leaving. Subsequently, I discovered that, by doing so, I had made things worse for them than I had thought. I did not want to impose my grief on them so I went to live near a community of nuns who gave me companionship and helped me contain my grief. Later on they helped to train me for the life I now live.

At first I could not go anywhere where Leo and I had been together, without crying. I did not enjoy going to new places or meeting new people. I was afraid of crowds. I did not like going out at night because it meant coming home to an empty house. The coming of my first grandchild, nine months after Leo's death, propelled me into some happiness, but I felt guilty about it. It was not until I entered the recovery period that I really started to feel cheerful again and began to make judgements that were not influenced by the effects of grief.

During the whole of this period of bereavement, survivors may find that their relationships with other relatives, friends and professional colleagues are adversely affected. Certainly that was true for me. Other people treated me differently from the way they had when Leo was alive. Some assumed I was now free to engage in casual sexual relationships. Others appeared to be somewhat afraid that I might make a bid for their husbands. Being, at the time, someone who was living on automatic pilot, overseen by an internal controller, I observed these changes in my relationships with amused detachment. This emotional remoteness did save me from being precipitated into a dangerous relationship during the time of impaired judgement. It also helped me to respond more appropriately to professional advisors, who assumed that I was an idiot in regard to monetary affairs, and to salesmen, who considered me a prime target for exploitation.

FAITH DURING BEREAVEMENT

Knowing that I am a practising Christian, friends have often asked me whether my faith helped me during the period of my bereavement? The answer is that my faith helped me inasmuch as it was against suicide, but it was not the prime factor in my decision to remain alive.

My children were. Otherwise faith did not really come into the equation at first.

I had no sense of my husband's resurrection life, no comforting 'visits' from him. Religious observance of any kind became another robot-like occupation. I had gone to church before my husband's death. I continued to do so afterwards. I continued to pray, by that time in my life being habituated to prayer. I had no direct apprehension of God, but then that was nothing new. Religious faith for me had never been a 'felt' experience. For many years prior to this major bereavement, prayer had been a self-emptying, waiting on God. I had little expectation of being filled with knowledge or a sentient experience of God; I did, however, believe that God could act if and when God wanted to act.

In my own case, faith was no more comforting than it had been before my bereavement, nor did I lose it in any way. That is not so for many people to whom I have talked as doctor and priest. Faith can disappear out of the window in an instant, consumed by anger with God for allowing such an unjust death. Faith in God's very existence can be severely strained by cruel deaths of all kinds. Initially, it may be difficult to express anger with God. It may be nearly impossible to express one's doubts about God's existence to other people. At the same time, a person's perception of God's nature can be totally distorted by grief. It is not at all uncommon for a survivor to think of God as a kind of malevolent puppeteer who positively enjoys a 'cat and mouse' game with human beings. Intellectually, one may know that God is not like that, but that does not help much at the time. Feelings, if one can still feel at all, prevail.

Anger with God may come early or comparatively late in a survivor's recovery. Experience prompts me to think that expressed anger with God, at the disaster that has befallen both the dead and the survivors, may be a small sign that the recovery period is imminent, especially if feelings have been suppressed for any length of time. I am always pleased when such anger erupts. Human beings revolt against death because they are not able to control it. It is right that they should blame a God perceived as the great Controller and Despot. The fact that their image of God is a false one is immaterial. Such distortions of image may serve a purpose. They need not be contradicted immediately. Volcanic anger can be cathartic and mark the beginning of more realistic attitudes towards God and oneself. It can certainly assist recovery.

Some people never experience that kind of anger with God at all. Their faith in resurrection life, in the continued existence of the dead person, in the communion of saints, seems to enhance their ability to face bereavement and life as a survivor with equanimity. There have been times in my life when I have witnessed this kind of serenity in others with amazement, even with suspicion.

Such misgiving may be justified. People who find themselves 'living on a high' after the death of a beloved relative or child may be defending themselves against natural grief. They may be suppressing feelings of guilt and anger which will emerge at a later date, sometimes in an explosive and damaging way. They may even be repressing them, unaware that the feelings are still operating at a subconscious level and causing unexplained physical symptoms.

I do not want to deny that personal faith is a comfort to many, a source of strength to some. It seems to me that God, my kind of God anyway, deals with people according to their need. In my own case, severe bereavement stripped me of false notions about the nature of God. It forced me to look at what I meant when I recited the Nicene Creed of the Christian Church and said the words, 'I look for the resurrection of the dead, and the life of the world to come' (BCP: Church in Wales). Had I not been who God made me, God might have dealt with me very much more gently and given me assurance, blessed assurance. That, however, was not God's way with me. I shall be exploring this dimension of faith in more depth in a later chapter.

Acceptance of loss, adaptation and making a fresh start

I have almost spoken of this phase of the grief process as recovery, but in truth it is impossible to recover what has been permanently lost. Grief of the magnitude I am speaking about can, however, lead to acceptance of one's loss and a willingness to make a fresh start. The willingness to make that fresh start as a survivor is marked in very small ways at its outset. In my own case, it began with moments of unsought happiness. These coalesced, in time, into quite long periods of being able to feel pleasure. At first these times came when I was alone. I found enjoyment in reading that had hitherto escaped me. I could listen to music without weeping. I could enjoy walking out of doors. Later, I began to feel intense pleasure in being with my children and grandchildren. Eventually, laughter – natural laughter with friends – came back into my life. I began to be able to adjust, to enjoy living alone, to stop shrinking from contact with other people.

Full entry into a new phase of life was marked by the return of the natural emotions of anxiety, anger, frustration, high spirits. Some three years into the grief process I found I was beginning to be able to make sensible judgements, but the resumption of full responsibility for my actions was delayed until the fourth year. I did not, and do not, repudiate any of the decisions I made during my period of impaired decision making. The mistakes, such as they were, contributed to my growth as a human being. When the fresh start 'set in', so to speak, I found that all kinds of good things had been happening as a result of my many errors of judgement, almost without my knowing it. Indeed, I would go so far as to say that, without those errors, I could not have learnt as much as I now know I did. Some of my actions and behaviour during the period of severe bereavement were incomprehensible and disturbing to my family, close friends and spiritual advisors. I am sorry for the hurt that I caused to all of these people during those years, but I am not sorry at all that they happened. They were part of growth, part of the wisdom I needed to acquire if I was to live the rest of my life in a creative way.

It takes courage to enter a new period of life, as many people besides myself have found. Initially, people often find themselves feeling guilty at being happy, looking forward to each day, enjoying a fresh start of any kind. These feelings have to be set aside gently. The instinct for survival is great: in the end most people do experience a sense of gratitude that they are still alive and able to contribute positively to the life of their families, friends and the community in which they live.

Once I had entered this phase of the grief process, I found myself able to make informed decisions again. The resulting change of direction in my mode of life – I left the religious community I had joined and started living alone again – seemed abrupt, but in reality it had been germinating for a long time. The decisions were painful, both to myself and to my former companions in the convent, but they had to be made. They grew out of my time in community and I shall always be grateful for the things I learnt from my sisters in religion, but I could not live as I am living now had I stayed with them. Moreover, although I had wanted to live as I am living now for a very long time, I could not have done so unless I had learnt what I needed to learn within the environment of a convent. A period in prison, a mental hospital or a prolonged illness of any sort might, as I well know, have accomplished the same end.

Bereavement after disasters other than physical death

So far, I have focused on physical bereavement because it is the most obvious condition in which a person finds themselves alive after death. Yet there are many other disasters in life that provoke much the same reaction. Divorce, a broken engagement, the disappearance of a loved friend, the loss of a job, sudden disgrace, imprisonment, injustice, the loss of money or home, or the death of animals can all lead to the same symptoms and signs in those who have to go on living after such events. Moreover, the ill effects of having to go on living when one would rather be dead, or at least able to go to sleep 'for a hundred years' to escape the pains of life, may be just as great as they can be in bereavement after the physical death of other human beings.

The process of adaptation to loss and successful survival is very individual. I have sketched my own personal experience and shown how it fits into, or does not fit into, the general pattern laid down by experts after considerable research. In doing that, I do not want to deny that each person is unique in their responses, but I think that human beings do have certain affinities, and that it can be helpful to see how alike, as well as how different, we are to one another.

In the next chapter I want to look at some of the ways in which people can find strength to survive disaster and to move from mere existence into successful survival and recovery of health and happiness.

4

Finding the strength to survive

'For there is hope for a tree, if it is cut down, that it will sprout again,
and that its shoots will not cease.'
(Job 14:7)

Looking back on my life, I see that I have met disasters with a kind of
dogged determination not to be defeated by them. One of the
questions that has exercised me throughout has been, 'Why have I
survived when others have not?' The complementary question to that
one is, 'Why does anyone survive?'

These next two chapters are an exploration into those two
questions. In this chapter, I have tried to reflect on the human, innate
factors that have helped me and other people to survive disaster. In the
next, I examine the help that it is possible to get from outside oneself.
The two chapters cover some of the ground we have already explored
but their perspective is different. They are written by someone who is
no longer a reluctant survivor but who is now confident that survival
can lead to health. I have begun to tackle the two questions referred to
above, although I have not yet found all the answers.

The last chapter was primarily concerned with the effects on one
person of one kind of disaster, that of the physical death of close
relatives. That kind of death takes place at a particular time. It is a
'one-off' event. Death ends one phase of life and begins another. It has
consequences for survivors which become obvious as life continues,
but these are relatively easy to document and understand. In this
chapter, however, I want to take the effects of other disasters, and of
continuing disappointment, as the principal objects of my reflections.
This is a more complex area of life to explore since, in so far as it is
possible, it involves understanding oneself and the genesis of one's
own temperament.

Like many other people whom I know, life has not always gone smoothly for me. I have not fulfilled the early promise in my professional career as a doctor. This was largely because I was not single-minded enough. I wanted to do other things besides medicine, and I did. Medicine has always been in competition with my life as a wife and mother, but, at various times, it has also been in competition with my life as a Christian called to the priesthood and the religious life.

People who look at my life from outside see a polymath who tries to do too many things and succeeds in doing none of them excellently. So they have been disappointed. 'Why can't you settle down to being a general practitioner, a wife and a mother?' several of my mentors and friends said to me when I first approached the Church of England to see if I could train to be a deaconess as well as a doctor. 'Why do you need to train in psychiatry to be a good general practitioner?' others said when I left general practice for a time to get some further training in psychiatry. 'Why do you want to go back to being a nun when you're a deacon doing useful work in a parish?' one of the disappointed parishioners in my local Christian community asked me, on hearing that I was about to leave the parish for life in a religious community. Why indeed?

Part of the answers to these uncomfortable questions and perceptions of outsiders lie in my family background and genes, part in the pursuit of a way of life that could enable me to survive the successive and repetitive disappointments of life. In my efforts to survive various setbacks I have managed to discover how disparate and sometimes warring elements in my own personality could be integrated. I have also found ways of encouraging other people to live more happily with the natures they have inherited.

The blessing of genes

My ancestors on both sides of the family were a motley company. They included globetrotters, medical doctors, eminent Anglican clerics, salesmen and travellers. Nearly all of them could speak many languages and cross cultures with relative ease. They adapted to each different situation in life and, because they could do that, many of them managed to survive exile, adversities, reversals of fortune and wars, before finally dying of unpleasant scourges such as typhus, tuberculosis and cancer, or of sheer exhaustion after walking hundreds of miles into exile.

My grandmother, Victoria, was a member of the large family of an English doctor, Octavius Temple, who practised his art as physician to the Sultan of Turkey. Octavius' brother, Frederick, was a clergyman, eventually destined to become Archbishop of Canterbury in 1896. It was from this side of the family, through my maternal grandmother and mother, that I inherited some of my physical features, such as my large nose, intellectual abilities and a marked tendency to obesity.

It was from my grandmother that I inherited my religious mind; of that I am in no doubt. But I inherited more than that. Recently I read a biography of Archbishop Frederick Temple.[1] In it, there is reference to his habits of studying. It appears that, when he was an undergraduate at Oxford in 1841, he went to bed at about half past ten, habitually waking at four in the morning, or even 'sometimes by three, without any fatigue, and without even an alarum to awake me'.[2] Just over a hundred years later, without knowing anything about that side of my family, I was doing exactly the same, and, to this day, my best work is done between the hours of three and eight in the morning. Like Temple again, during the evening, I 'tend to do my easy work, and anything which does not require much attention, as I do not like to work very hard in the evening'.[3] Later on in the biography there is reference to Temple's capacity for sustained concentration. On one occasion, when he had to complete an important report for the Schools Enquiry Commission (1864–88), he wrote continuously for thirty-six hours, 'having tea brought to him at intervals, and the printer's devil in constant attendance'.[4] I, too, have that capacity, and, with others, have worked in similar fashion during the drafting of reports. It also appears that Frederick Temple had immense physical energy and stamina, coupled with an unusual ability to ignore physical fatigue. That, too, is a gift I have inherited through the Temple genes, although I have found it to be a dubious gift. Like him, I exhaust people with less physical energy than myself. Like him, I sometimes unwittingly make people feel inadequate simply because I can keep going when they are ripe for rest or sleep. Like him, I irritated people when I was younger because I could do so many things at one time. But there you are. Our genes are an integral part of ourselves. They cannot be changed and must be incorporated into a full enjoyment of one's life and personality. That is not to say that all actions are determined by one's genes. I do not believe that, but I do believe it is important to understand and work *with* one's given personality rather than against it.

My mother was a seventh child. From her I inherited my sixth, seventh and eighth senses, those supersensitive antennae which enable some people to pick up non-verbal communication and memory traces from the past, and also to anticipate certain events in people's lives. I also inherited a quick mind, a passionate nature, a vigorous sense of humour and an ability to deal with hardships, sufferings and frustrations. From her, too, I inherited a remarkable capacity to reconcile the apparently irreconcilable features in my own personality. I owe my mother a great deal else, but those are the main features of her character that later found expression in me, her only child.

My paternal grandfather was an English egg merchant who emigrated to Russia, where he bettered himself. He learnt to speak many languages. He raised a family. He acquired a status in Russia than he would never have had in England. That was how his family became intimate friends with my grandmother's family. My father, his brother and sister, were always in and out of my maternal grandmother's home. My father and mother virtually grew up together.

It was from my father, as well as from my maternal line, that I inherited a stocky build and a tendency to gain weight. Both of us found it necessary to eat far less than other people to maintain our normal weight. Even moderate overindulgence resulted in massive obesity.

From him, too, I inherited a tendency to addiction. Sadly, it led my father to alcoholism, for a large part of his adult life. Mercifully, for me, my adolescent contempt for his way of life led me in the opposite direction and kept me abstemious in the matter of drink and drugs until I could find ways, other than contempt, of remaining sober and away from the many addictive drugs to which I had easy access as a medical practitioner.

It was from my father that I inherited the genes for depression. I have been told that my paternal grandmother suffered from menopausal melancholia at one time, and I have certainly known myself to be ill with depression and in need of medical help from time to time, but my father never admitted to his needs. He might have had an easier life if he could have received help. He never did, but I was more fortunate. I did get help, and eventually discovered that hard physical work and intense mental creativity afforded some protection against that terrible condition.

It must have been from my father that I also inherited some genes for courage and tenacity of purpose. There is, I think, no doubt about my father's courage. His name surfaces in many books about the British Intelligence Services during and immediately after the First World War, when he was a colleague of men like Bruce Lockhart and Sidney Reilly. He spoke many languages, had many disguises, lived in constant fear of betrayal and often sought my mother's help as a go-between. When the 1914–18 war was over, he eventually wrote two books about his life as an Intelligence agent of that period, *Go Spy the Land* and *Dreaded Hour*.[5] Since, as I have already said, I only recall meeting my father twice during my formative years, once when I was eleven years old and once when I was eighteen, most of my information about him came from a surreptitious reading of these two books, which I found in the home of his sister, my Aunt Marguerite. I found the books when I was thirteen years old but, by that time, I had developed a fierce loyalty to my mother and could scarcely confess to a secret admiration for this brave man inside the pages of what felt like a fairytale.

Since I had so little contact with him during my childhood I cannot possibly have learnt from him in any way, other than through my genes, how to overcome naked fear with the kind of pride that passes for natural courage. Nor can I detect that tenacity of purpose which is part of my own character in any other of my many ancestors on my mother's side.

Knowing about these particular genes has been helpful to me. They explain some of my peculiarities and makes these more intelligible. Such understanding has also helped me to like myself better, since I now know that I can accept myself as I am. I am not a determinist. I believe in the possibility of change and in God's grace. So I have found that I can modify any ill effects my physique and temperament may have on other people. I can, I think, now use the relative insomnia and abundance of energy more wisely.

The blessing of shock in the immediacy of disaster

I have already written briefly about the effects of shock stemming from the disaster of anticipated or real bereavement. Physical shock is an internal bodily response to great stress. If, for instance, people are gravely injured in a car accident, their bodies immediately respond by a fall in blood pressure. This fall in blood pressure means that the victims will lose colour from their faces, become clammy and cold with sweat, will feel faint and may become unconscious. Provided that the heart is still able to pump some blood to the brain this response to severe stress is beneficial. The body cannot maintain an upright posture and the shocked person falls to the ground. All bodily movements are reduced to a minimum. The autonomic nervous system, that part of the nervous system that is not under the control of the will, automatically diverts blood from the periphery to the vital central organs of the body like the brain. This means that quite serious peripheral wounds do not bleed at all. Arteries may be severed by the ragged amputation of a limb, but the arteries in the stump simply contract instead of bleed; at any rate, until the immediate physical shock is over.

Physical shock results in a loss of consciousness, or impaired consciousness, and this is the body's way of protecting the individual from immediate death. It also serves to cushion the emotional shock of the disaster, whatever that might be. That is why those who give first aid to others are taught to let someone who has fainted lie flat, possibly raising their feet above their head so that the blood can drain more easily towards the head.

Shock is a state that follows insult to the body but it can also happen after severe emotional injury. That is why caring professionals often invite people to sit down before hearing bad news. That is why caring relatives instinctively take over many of the household duties of a bereaved person. Some sit with the shocked person. Others answer doorbells, pick up the telephone, welcome friends who have come to offer their condolences, fend off unnecessary intrusion, make cups of tea, deal with the documentation, arrange the funeral.

Immediate physical shock passes but emotional shock persists for much longer. Bereavement nearly always produces shock, but exactly the same process can happen to people who find themselves summarily dismissed. Shock, disbelief, early signs of anger can be seen on the faces of employees, who come into work one morning expecting to work as usual, and find that they have been made redundant overnight. On occasions, television records the cruel truth, and the world looks on, hoping that the same awful fate will not befall them the next day. Bad news of any sort can precipitate this kind of physical response.

Bad domestic news can be one of the most traumatic events in a person's life. The solicitor's letter that arrives one morning to tell someone that their spouse has filed for a divorce can precipitate severe shock and disbelief. The note on a table which tells a mother that her teenage son has decided to leave home can produce the same effect. An incredibly rude and angry letter from a friend who has taken offence at something one thought was an innocent remark can be quite devastating. These traumatic events are made worse if the recipient of the bad news had no idea what was coming.

Anticipation, however, does not always diminish the impact of bad news. I can remember an occasion when I applied for a medical post that I wanted very much and which I thought I deserved because I had been 'acting up' for some months and had done the work well. For weeks before the interview I knew in my bones that I was not going to get the job. There was a better-qualified contender for it and she had more experience. Nevertheless, the shock when the news came was very real. Failure to get the post meant that I would not get any rise in pay; I would have to work on in a subordinate position. I would have to hand over precious work to an incoming stranger. My responsibilities, to which I had become accustomed, would be reduced. Shock, which lasted for a few days, cushioned the news and rendered me incapable of action that might have precipitated a decision to resign altogether. I returned to work and acted automatically for some weeks until my replacement arrived to take up the post that I had briefly held. By that time, I had been able to accept the truth and adjust to it. I did not leave my job. When the next senior post was advertised I applied for it, and this time was successful.

Dreadful natural disasters, such as floods, hurricanes, earthquakes and volcanic eruptions produce shock on a large scale. Those of us who are not directly involved are appalled by the immediate after-effects of such terrible events. Those who remain alive after such catastrophes may wander around for days not knowing what to do. Children get separated from their parents and parents fail to remember that their child exists. Some adults cannot react emotionally at all. They just sit where they were when the disaster that killed or injured their relatives and neighbours first struck. They are clearly in a dazed condition. They do not eat, drink, cry, forage for food. Other adults become possessed by huge energy. They are desperate to find missing relatives and friends. They scrabble in the rubble, search frantically in mud and piles of earth, refuse to rest even for a moment. They exhaust themselves in a hopeless search, or become elated when one person is brought out of the debris alive, even though they have by this time realized that their own relatives and friends are dead.

Shock takes away a person's ability to act decisively. In that, it can be of benefit. Those who accompany anyone who is in a state of emotional shock should not hurry to bring the shocked person out of it. Automatism, numbness of feeling and adherence to dull routine can cushion the effects of the disaster. Shock can temporarily prevent someone from coming to the full realization of its consequences for his or her life. The benefit of physical and emotional shock, even if it is prolonged is, however, usually comparatively short-lived. The ability to make decisions will return after a variable length of time. Such capacity is often accompanied by an upsurge of grief or anger, or both. The most dangerous period in a survivor's life has begun.

The blessing of courage

All survivors need courage to go on living. Paradoxically, however, it also takes courage to make a decision to end one's own life. Courage is an innate disposition. Many of us, contemplating some of the awful things that happen to other people, about which we hear through the media, think of ourselves as cowards. 'I could never do that,' we say when we watch acts of heroic rescue on television or read about them in our daily paper. 'I know I'd never be able to go into a burning building to rescue someone, even if it was my own child,' we might confess. Yet few of us actually know what we would or would not do until disaster happens. Then we act according to our genetic inheritance, our training during the period of our development into adult life and our beliefs.

Courage is brought out by motive. A mother might want to die when she is widowed at an early age and is left impoverished and with young children to bring up. Despite her longing for the oblivion of death she may find the courage to go on living for the sake of her children. Alternatively, a father might decide that he cannot go on living without his wife. It takes a different form of courage to plan and carry out the murder of his surviving children and his own suicide. However much we might deplore such actions, or attribute them to a mental breakdown, there are certain cases in which we still have to respect the motive that prompted such behaviour. We naturally wish that the father had not emerged from his state of shock to the point where he was capable of killing himself and his children. We still have to admit that it took courage to do it, even if that courage seems to us an ultimate act of cowardice.

Death is not the only disaster that can produce a desire for oblivion. The shame of being unjustly dismissed or made redundant through no fault of one's own can upset the balance of a person's mind and precipitate actions that would not be taken in other circumstances. Divorce, the loss of a home through fire, the sudden loss of all one's invested money, a terrible row with a member of one's family – all these, and many more events – can result in a strong urge for death.

None of us knows precisely what makes survivors of disasters decide to live or die. In many people, the instinct to survive is so strong that this tilts them in favour of life. In others, a deathwish alters the balance. Usually, there is a complex interplay between innate characteristics and external assistance. If the balance is right, people afflicted by disaster will survive. They may even develop new and more satisfying lifestyles and find themselves more whole than they ever thought would be possible. If the balance between innate personality and external help goes awry, then the victims of disaster may die of causes immediately related to the disaster. They may succumb to stress-related illnesses or the urge to commit suicide.

There are some forms of death, however, that are more subtle than physical death. A person with a strong instinct towards death can unconsciously choose to reside in bitterness rather than choose to forgive and live. This sometimes happens, for instance, and very understandably so, when a child has been killed by a drunken driver, or raped and killed. One or both parents may find themselves locked into grief, anger and bitter resentment. Although they go on living, their whole outlook on life is coloured by this one terrible event. Indeed, they may become so lost in grief and depression that they are quite unable to care for each other and for their surviving children. It is useless to tell such people to 'get a move on'. They cannot. If they could, they would. Good genes and internal qualities of character will not, by themselves, produce the desired result of a positive attitude towards life. External help is often needed before those who feel themselves to be the 'living dead' can rediscover their zest for life.

Before I turn to those factors, however, there are two other internal factors which help survivors of a disaster to go on living. The first of these is anger.

The happiness of creative anger

Anger *can* be a most wonderfully creative factor in the lives of survivors, both those who are survivors after physical bereavement and those to whom life has been cruel in other ways. Not all forms of anger, however, are creative and it is, I think, necessary to distinguish carefully between destructive and creative anger.

Destructive anger

There are many different forms of destructive anger. There is blind rage that suddenly overwhelms a person, is sometimes uncontrollable and can splurge out in a torrent of physical or verbal abuse that does great damage, not only to the target, but also to the one who is seized with this kind of anger. This damage may be exceptionally grave if a person with a quick temper lashes out at another with a slow fuse.

There is slow, simmering anger that persists long after the original provocation. This kind of anger can alienate relationships with one's partners, colleagues and friends. In one way it seems to be a more dangerous form of destructive anger than the flare-up of a quick temper that is over almost as soon as it starts. This is because the person with a slow response can brood for a very long time over incidents which have been long since forgotten by the person with a more quick rising temper.

Most difficult of all the destructive angers to contend with is concealed or displaced anger. This kind of anger occurs most commonly among people who are afraid of the strength of their own emotions. It may happen to those who, in their youth, have learnt to suppress anger through fear: they may have had to restrain their anger against some powerful adult figure who was dominant during their early development. The anger turns inwards and turns itself into guilt, depression and passivity. This was the way I went.

Initially, when I was a child and young person, I could, and did, express destructive anger. If I was angry with my mother, I would break something that she had given me. If I was angry with a teacher, I could taunt her with my wit. If I took a dislike to fellow pupils, or, later, other medical students, I had a way of using my eyes that would make them want to put distance between themselves and me. This kind of hostile behaviour persisted almost until I qualified as a doctor. I learnt to control it, as I was ashamed of it. Later, under the influence of the Christian faith, I suppressed any manifestation of anger, even righteous anger, for many years. Unconsciously, I turned it against myself through becoming depressed.

People who are afflicted by this form of concealed anger tend to blame themselves for things that go wrong, even if it is perfectly obvious that they are not responsible for the error or disaster. Since they are afraid of any strong emotion, particularly anger against someone they are supposed to love, they become depressed. Reactive depression, for instance, is a common manifestation in people who have been unjustly dismissed or rejected for promotion. They should be angry, but they are afraid to be angry or unable to feel anger. Instead they become depressed. They punish themselves for their apparent failures. Some of the people afflicted in this way become passive. They are quite unable to appeal against an unjust dismissal, take employers to court for compensation, or do anything but run away from the whole wretched situation. Self-confidence and self-esteem go out of the window and it takes a long time for these qualities to be regained.

Occasionally, people who are passive and depressed will react with unexpected volcanic anger. I can recall an incident in my own life where I was rebuked by the head of my department and told to apologize for a fault I had not committed. By this time I was well into middle age. At the time I was afraid of being dismissed, and, since I was the only source of income in the family, I was precipitated into acute panic. I was meek at the time of the rebuke. I did as I was told and apologized. As soon as my superior was out of the room, I found myself shaking, so much so that I was prostrate for several minutes. Only later did I realize that the anger had at last surfaced in a healthy way.

That upsurge of anger, was, in the end, liberating. Once I recognized its presence and its genesis, I was able to alter my behaviour towards this particular person and ultimately towards other authority figures. They could no longer subdue me in the same way. They could no longer bully me into submission. They could not use the threat of dismissal as a way of bringing me to heel. I was prepared to leave. I found freedom from guilt and depression because, almost for the first time in my life, I could admit to myself that there were occasions when I should be angry with other people and not take the blame myself for their errors and injustices. I had begun to discover the freedom of creative anger. It should be noted that I had only begun. From that time until today, I have frequently relapsed into a 'doormat' state; a state of submissive self-reproach which enables its victims to be bullied, even terrorized, into compliance. At least, however, I know what I am doing now, and can sometimes find better ways of reacting to injustice.

Creative anger

In order to outline the characteristics of creative anger and some of its differences from destructive anger, I need to share my own slow movement from the passive destructive form of anger to its more active creative form. The latter has been an important factor in my own life and development as a person. Initially, it emerged alongside guilt and depression in small and abortive spurts. Yet, even in those small upsurges, the creative energy of anger did help me to survive many repeated disappointments and frustrations of life, particularly that of rejection because of my being a woman.

I did not really notice any major disadvantage in being a woman when I was young. I entered a profession that was more interested in my intellect than in my gender. The main disadvantage in being a woman was that the medical career structure was heavily biased in favour of men. However, when I left convent life in 1957 and decided to get married I was not worried about status. I settled happily for marriage and general practice, two modes of life that agreed well with each other.

General practice in England, at that time, was a profession that did not offer women equal opportunities, but it did offer them equal pay, if not equal pension rights. I scarcely noticed any difficulty in becoming a principal in general practice. I was well paid and well treated by my colleagues in the London suburb where I worked for the next ten years. I experienced a few minor problems, chief of which was the fact that I could not be responsible for my own debts. I could not sign hire-purchase agreements in my own name. If I wanted to make any major purchase on extended credit, I had to obtain the signature of my husband on the contract. That distressed me but, as there was no way round the law of the land at the time, I came to terms with such difficulties.

I might never have understood what being a woman could mean in a society where sex discrimination was rampant in regard to pay and equal opportunities had I not become aware of the plight of many of the women who were not medical doctors. Among them were those women who made up the large mass of low-paid, low-status workers in society, some of whom came to me as their family doctor. While I could not, even in early middle age, get angry on my own behalf, I found that I could feel some anger at the plight of other people. I used it to encourage them to stand up for themselves and to stand together in solidarity against reactionary forces in society. I gave support whenever and wherever I could, though in a rather quiet, passive and non-demanding way.

Then things changed. They did so because I had one of my volcanic spurts of creative anger, though I could not have named it as such at the time. In 1970, I was 44 years old. I was a well-established family doctor in partnership with four other doctors in a South London suburb. I was happily married and my family was complete. Yet I was also feeling increasingly angry at the treatment of women in British society (I was still ignorant of the worse plight of women in some overseas countries) and similarly concerned at the way in which the churches were treating their women. By 1970, the pot, so to speak, had been simmering for over three years. In that year, the volcano of creative anger inside me began to 'go active' in a sustained way. It started to channel itself into a determination to overcome large obstacles that stood in the way of women's work being valued as it should be by church and state. Creative anger had begun to overcome my fear of it becoming destructive.

During the preceding three years I had trained as a deaconess of the Church of England. I had experienced the effects of being under-valued by the church purely because I was a woman. My fellow students were, on the whole, kind beyond description but some of my teachers were insensitive to the difficulties I faced due to being a lone woman in a company of some fifty students, all of whom were in training for the ordained ministry of the church. On the contrary, they exacerbated the problem. For the whole of my first year's training, for instance, I was not allowed to stay overnight at the place in Surrey that was used for our monthly residential weekends. Instead, I had to commute back and forth on a daily basis. It was physically exhausting. It was also humiliating to think that I, a happily married woman with four young children, was regarded as a potential danger to my fellow students.

I do not suppose that my trainers meant to be cruel in any way. They just lacked imagination. They did Christian women a great service, however, for the treatment meted out to me during my student years in this and other ways, turned my husband, who had initially been sceptical, into an ardent supporter of women's ordination. My anger, and his, fuelled our joint determination to endure whatever we had to endure for the sake of getting me through the course. All the energy of anger was focused and directed towards overcoming a multitude of obstacles that might have defeated two less determined people.

That first year of training also made me realize that injustice could not be combated by destructive anger towards a system that regarded human beings as stereotypes instead of as persons who needed help and encouragement. Injustice had to be fought by using anger creatively. My own experiences as a woman in a man's world were preparing me for wider work in society.

When we finished our training in 1970, my fellow students were all ordained into the diaconate of the Church of England. A year later they became priests. Neither of those options was open to me. Instead, I became a deaconess, a trained and commissioned lay-woman. As such, my duties in church would be restricted to an assistant role. I was made a deaconess in December 1970 and I continued to work as a family doctor. Neither the Church of England nor I had any idea of what that would mean in the future.

In 1972 the British government of the day published a green paper in which they said that they would stop paying family allowances directly to women. Instead, they proposed paying them through men's pay packets. I, and one of our practice health visitors, were dismayed about this suggestion. We were working on a large housing estate where many people were economically disadvantaged. We knew that many men would simply not pay over that precious allowance to their wives and partners. We decided to join a protest march from Hyde Park to Westminster.

Eager to go with other Christian women, I rang up some twenty Christian organizations to see if I could join them. None of them were going. One expressed the opinion of all when she said: 'No, I'm sorry, we don't support women like that.'

'Like what?' I said. 'Well, you know; communists and lesbians and feminist "bra-burners".'

I did not know. So I decided to go and find out. I also decided to go in my navy-blue deaconess cassock. My presence at the march and subsequent rally drew other Christian women to my side, but it also intrigued some of the other women, notably Mary Stott, editor of *The Guardian's* women's page, who knew that the established Church of England's attitude towards its women members was harmful to many women outside the church. Before very long, I found myself working with Mary and her colleagues in Women in Media. Our objective was to raise women's profiles in the media and to improve women's opportunities and pay in general.

This was the beginning of ten years' public work on behalf of women in society. This was carried out while simultaneously trying to persuade the worldwide Anglican Church to ordain women to the threefold historic ministries of deacons, priests and bishops. It was also the beginning of a great expansion in my own knowledge and understanding of the more serious disadvantages experienced by women in less affluent countries of the world than my own. During this time, I travelled widely and met many women from Third World countries.

During the years 1970 to 1993 we, who were campaigners on behalf of women's social right to equal opportunities and equal pay for equal work, took a lot of risks. Having very little money, a condition common among women in society, and virtually no power, we pursued what we thought to be the most effective way of bringing the plight of women to the politicians' notice. We courted publicity for our cause. Since many of us were employed by the media we got it, and we used it to encourage all political parties to support the Equal Pay and Equal Opportunities bills which, at the start of that period were beginning their tortuous progress through the British parliamentary process.

In 1974, I stood for parliament in a marginal seat to gain publicity for our precious bills. My agent was Jewish. One of my chief supporters was a communist. Another was a prospective Conservative candidate for parliament. Several were ardent Labour supporters. Several were Liberals. The reason I was chosen to be the 'front woman' for this cross-party political campaign was, very simply, that I belonged to the then respectable profession of medicine. I was also happily married and a churchgoing Christian. My colleagues thought that I was the kind of person that had a supportive husband and family. They reckoned that my credibility could not be destroyed by media allegations about my personal and private life. In that they were right, but neither the women who persuaded me to stand on their behalf in the 1974 General Election, nor I, had noticed my Achilles heel: my tendency to revert to self-destructive anger when I was experiencing rejection.

I probably should have recognized that I was sensitized to rejection by my childhood experiences. I should have realized that my Christian faith was bound up with the belief that God loved and accepted women as his close friends and disciples. To me it seemed natural to expect the church to show the same love. I was mistaken. When Christians I respected rejected women for the ordained ministry, which many of them were vigorously doing at the time, they were making it clear that they did not believe that women were fit persons to represent God in any way. Some of my Christian friends also thought that my secular work was harming the cause of women's ordination. My creative anger began to turn into destructive anger. It turned inward.

During that May campaign, the rest of that year and the next year, 1975, when the Equal Opportunity Acts and the Equal Pay Act came on to the statute book, I steadily lost self-confidence and self-esteem. The bouts of guilt and depression lengthened. I saw many other women suffering loss of faith, loss of belief in themselves, profound disillusionment with the church of their birth. I saw some breaking down under the strain. I was saddened when many of my Christian friends decided to leave the Church of England and did so. I did not, however, break under the strain myself until after the adverse vote against the ordination of women in 1978.

By that time, most of my own secular political work was done. By that time, also, I and a small band of Christian men and women from all denominations were using publicity to focus attention on the issue of women's ordination to the diaconate and priesthood of the Anglican Church in England. Many of my Christian friends disapproved of the worship services, the demonstrations, the all-night vigils of witness and the television programmes we used for publicity purposes. Some accused us of 'putting the cause back' by fifty, even a hundred, years.

In November, 1978, Elsie Baker, an older, very well-liked and respected, deaconess, joined with me and others in keeping vigil all night before the day of the debate on the ordination of women. I remember with affection the friendly police who watched over us, the hot cups of coffee brought to us by well-wishers, the sudden appearance of Dr John Robinson and some other notable churchmen 'on the line'. We were reeling with tiredness by the time we climbed into the gallery in Church House to listen to the five-hour debate.

Scarcely two hours went by before I knew that things were going to go wrong for us. The atmosphere in the gallery was hostile. The arguments on the floor of the debating chamber tended to be frivolous, even slightly 'jokey' at times. I spent the remaining three hours in a crouched position praying. Gradually I became aware that some force inside me was pushing me to react to the expected negative vote. Words came into my head. They would not go away. They were: 'We asked you for bread and you gave us a stone.' They were a reference to the New Testament where Jesus asked a rhetorical question: 'Is there anyone among you who, if a child asks for bread, will give a stone? (Matthew 7:9). Jesus plainly expected the answer to be 'No'.

When the vote came through, I was ready. The media knew where I was in the hall. With Sue Dowell by my side, I stood up and shouted the words out as loudly as I could. To them I added words that Dr Michael Ramsey had uttered out of his disappointment at the failure of the Anglicans to ratify the Anglican–Methodist reunion scheme in 1969: 'Long live God.'

It was a very unladylike thing to do. The words were greeted with a gasp of horror, but they were not forgotten.

The next phase of the struggle had arrived, but I was not to be active in it for very long. After the vote I felt very defeated for a long time. I had lost friends through my activism and through my 'outrageous' behaviour in General Synod. I had become stereotyped. After the adverse vote I became unable to hold a calm and rational discussion about the role of women in the church. I was compelled by my own admission of this handicap to withdraw from all active efforts to enter into dialogue with adversaries and lukewarm supporters. I also knew that other, younger women, and many more of them, would need to front the next phase of the campaign rather than myself. Within the year, I left London and the media for the quieter regions of East Sussex. My work now, I knew, was to pray and to go on praying until I could regain my creative anger and not allow it to revert to the destructive kind.

It was to take me five more years to learn the lessons of nearly ten years of very active public life. Slowly and painfully I learnt, largely through the guidance of the Holy Spirit, to stop using anger destructively and to start using it creatively again. When I stopped turning the anger inwards and again began to accept that there was such a thing as righteous anger, I still found that I wanted to use it destructively: to lash out at those who had hurt me and so many of my friends, to treat them as they had treated us, to break off our friendship in revenge. To have done so might have given me some personal satisfaction but it would not have helped me to become a more whole person, one who could learn to love even those who reject my womanhood.

I mention all this to show how difficult it can be to use anger creatively. Even when one has begun to do so, it is difficult to sustain the momentum – to use the anger to stand in solidarity with others, to assist them in whatever way one can, to continue to educate and reform systems rather than attacking the individuals who are as trapped in the system as its victims.

Creative anger, of the kind I have described in my own experience, generates great energy. That energy can be put into sustained efforts to achieve justice, reform, renewal, the building up of individuals and communities. The energy of indignation at injustice can keep workers for peace and justice motivated for very long periods of time. Many of my friends in both secular and church circles knew that they would die before they had seen the fruits of their work, but they went on faithfully to their lives' end for the sake of their children and grandchildren. I hope to do the same.

Creative anger is an essential internal factor in survival. It has been described by those who have lived through the experience of being incarcerated in concentration camps and prisons during the Second World War, and by those who have survived oppressive political regimes. The 'will to live' has kept many patients alive when their medical condition seemed almost hopeless. That same determination has sometimes enabled men and women to survive the elements after shipwrecks, aeroplane crashes or breakdowns of vehicles in the desert.

If these inherent qualities of shock and creative anger are present in most, if not all, people, why is it that some of us exhibit a strong desire to live and the ability to grow through even the most terrible of disasters, while others give up and die, either physically or emotionally? In indicating some of the characteristics that help people to survive sustained and repeated personal rejection, I have become acutely aware that my own personality would have become severely distorted had I not had a strong value system, partly innate, partly acquired. I owe this to the factor of faith.

The blessing of faith

Faith is a word that evokes profound happiness in some people and a shudder in others, because, whenever the word is used, they usually think about faith as a religious concept. It may, of course, be that but faith can also be much wider and have no religious content at all.

In order to survive disaster, people need to believe that there is some purpose in their survival. The will to live is innate in most young people. In later adult life it diminishes in certain situations of severe illness, profound unhappiness, cataclysmic natural disaster, and in extreme old age. So where do we rediscover a sense of purpose? Where does faith come from? On what can we build new beginnings? In my experience, at least, internal qualities and external help are inseparable. None of us can go it alone. It is to sources of help in rekindling faith in the future that we now turn in the next chapter.

5

Finding help on the way

'Therefore I have uttered what I did not understand, things too
wonderful for me, which I did not know.'
(Job 42:3)

Building bridges with the help of faith

People like me, who do not have personal experience of cataclysmic
natural disasters, know that our own small traumas may feel
catastrophic to us, but we also know that they simply do not
compare to the terrible sufferings of some people about whom we
read, hear or see through radio and television.

Imagination helps us to understand what it was like for the five
polar explorers led by Captain Robert Falcon Scott who perished on
their way back from the South Pole in 1912.[1] Experience of thirst
enables us to empathize with those who find themselves stranded in a
desert, like the man rescued by the explorer missionaries, Eva and
Francesca French and Mildred Cable. They came across him in the
Gobi Desert on one of their treks in the early part of the twentieth
century. Despite the protests of their guides, who knew that picking
up an exhausted and dehydrated man would retard the progress of
their own caravan, the women tended the half-dead man and took
him with them to the next oasis. The man lived. The women thought
their action was quite reasonable. The indigenous guides continued to
think that the missionaries were either mad or irresponsible. They
could scarcely believe their own good fortune when they reached
water and safety.[2]

Such tales abound in the history of exploration, but they are also
common in contemporary life. Quite often it is possible to read about
someone who has been exposed to the elements and survived. While
writing this chapter, for instance, I opened the inside pages of my

newspaper and found a picture of a thirty-year-old climber called Jamie Andrew. It was taken during a climb of Ben Nevis. The reason it made the news was that the climber had no forearms and no lower legs. Some eighteen months previously he and his best friend, Jamie Fisher, had been climbing a thirteen-thousand-foot mountain, Les Droites, in the French Alps. A blizzard had trapped them for five days on a high ridge. Jamie Fisher died from exposure. Jamie Andrew was rescued but his frozen arms and lower limbs had to be amputated. In tribute to his friend, Jamie Andrew climbed Ben Nevis, the last mountain they had climbed together before their tragic accident. It took him five hours to reach the summit, but he did it, and the £5,500 he raised through the climb was given to the British Red Cross and Access, a charity that takes disabled people on holiday.[3]

Reading survival stories does not have quite the same effect as hearing about such an experience from a person first-hand. As a child of twelve, I can remember sitting in a wooden bungalow in Latvia while my tiny, thin, elderly grandmother told me about her own trek on foot from Moscow to Latvia in 1918. She and her eldest daughter had fled from the communist army during the early days of the Russian Revolution and had reached safety in Latvia. Her graphic description of the hardships of the journey, the cold, the lack of food, the sore blistered feet, the skin of her back rubbed sore by the straps of the bundle she carried on her back, impressed me greatly. When, after the end of the 1939–45 war, the news reached us of her death on another trek – this time from Latvia to Germany – I recalled our conversation in 1938 in vivid detail. Because she was a close relative I felt her death more keenly than I would have done had she been someone I met only through the pages of history books and media reports.

It was not, however, until my own family ground to a halt in the middle of a desert that I knew the magnitude of fear in such situations. Early in January 1960, Leo, my husband, Florence, our eldest child (then aged eighteen months) and Leo, our son (aged six weeks) were on our way from Odibo in Namibia to Omboloka, some ninety miles away. We travelled, as we always did, by a four-wheel-drive Land-Rover. We were accompanied, as we always were, by a Namibian guide. We had set out, as usual, in the very early morning to avoid the heat of the day. The Land-Rover was loaded up with adequate supplies of water and food. We carried the supply of medicine and dressings that I would use when we reached our destination. Visits to this distant outpost were a quarterly routine. On arrival, I would hold an open-air clinic lasting most of the afternoon. We would sleep in the Land-Rover. The following day, Leo would hold a service and I would hold another clinic before setting off for home.

The track was sand, and more sand. It was my turn to drive and we were coasting along at about ten miles an hour when the front wheel of the Land-Rover on the driver's side suddenly plunged into a deep soft pothole. My husband and our guide got out to dig us out. I, quite unworried at this time, retreated to the back of the vehicle to breastfeed my baby and to give my daughter a drink. An hour later we were still stuck fast in the sand. Our guide put his ear to the beaten-down track in front of our stricken vehicle and emerged from his lying-down position a few minutes later to tell us that 'help was coming'. 'They may be here in two hours,' he said. There was, of course, no sign of anyone at all in the deserted spot where we had come to grief. 'Two hours', in Namibian time, meant an unspecified 'sometime'.

By this time the morning sun was beating down upon us. We were thirsty but knew we had to conserve water for the children. They were fractious. There was virtually no wind to cool our hot skins. We lay down in the back of the car to conserve energy.

It has to be understood that I was in a postnatal phase of recovery from the birth of my son. My emotions were unstable. My imagination was lively. My husband, much more experienced a missionary than I, appeared to be unworried and was sitting quietly. He looked as if he was praying. I tried to do the same but utterly failed to do anything but feel afraid; not so much for myself, but for my two young children who could become dehydrated so easily in that climate.

I have to admit that 'faith in God' was but a nominal quality during the next few hours. Faith in the mysterious ways of south west Africa was more possible. Our Namibian guide's assertion that 'help was coming' seemed absurd to scientifically trained, rational ears. We had no radio contact with anyone, no telephone communication, no apparent means of telling anyone about our plight. I supposed that if we did not turn up at Omboloka on time a search party would be sent out. That was what African society deemed should be done, whatever the cost to the rescuers. That our African guide could put his ear to the ground and tell us that help was on its way, seemed impossible.

Some two hours later, and after several more sessions with his ear to the ground, our guide announced that help was indeed here. A small dust-cloud in the distance told us he was right. During those two hours I had run the gamut of fear for our family and arrived at a place where determination to survive outweighed that fear.

Where did that determination to live come from? Not, so far as I was aware, from my genes or courage or creative anger. Shock had not, in this instance, protected me at all from realizing the potential danger of our situation. Religious faith did not extend to thinking that God would act from 'his throne above the sky' to send help. An innate desire to live certainly contributed to my canny planning for survival. But faith, in the sense of trust in African ways and in an inner conviction that we would be rescued, was certainly operative. It dealt with the fear that had threatened to overwhelm me and set my mind free to plan for the time of waiting and beyond.

The six strong young men who appeared out of the sun, dug us out. After making sure that the Land-Rover was not the worse for its ordeal, they simply melted away again. We continued on our journey, arrived in the dark too late to hold a clinic, but received a warm welcome. The next morning it was 'work as usual'.

It is quite possible that we were never in as much danger as I thought we were at the time. What that personal experience made me understand, however, was the potency of fear in such situations. Fear can destroy logical thought. It can sap one's will to live, eroding faith and destroying hope. I am here using the word faith in the general sense used by the New Testament author of the book of Hebrews, 'Now faith is the assurance of things hoped for, the conviction of things not seen' (Hebrews 11:1).

Fear was, for me, the dominant feeling during the initial stages of our waiting to be rescued from a potentially dangerous situation in the desert. It could have overwhelmed me. I was fortunate in that it was overcome by faith. Faith did not take away the feeling of fear, but it lost its dominance in my mind. That kind of faith is universal.

As a medical doctor I have accompanied many people who have no religious faith at all, but they develop intense faith in their doctors and/or a particular regime of medication. They adopt a lifestyle which they think may cure them of cancer. They cling to a belief in other people's miracle cures. They hold on to a sense that there is still purpose in their lives, that they have something more to accomplish before they die. Faith of that kind is a potent spur to life. When it is gone, the person often dies very peacefully.

I can, for instance, recall a time when I met someone whom I will call Eva, a middle-aged woman who had cancer. She had been the mainstay of her husband who had been crippled with rheumatoid arthritis for many years.

In the early stages of her cancer, Eva carried on as usual. She underwent unpleasant treatment without a murmur of complaint. She believed that her purpose was to look after her husband and she would let nothing stand in the way of that task. She had no religious faith at all, but she was convinced that her destiny was to outlive her husband. When it became obvious to everyone around her that she was not going to do that, she still carried on as if she was well. Time and again she refused palliative hospital treatment. 'I won't come out of there again', she said to me. 'If you send me in, I shall die. Promise me that you'll not do that.'

I could not make that promise, but I reassured her that I would not act against her wishes unless her staying at home would impair the quality of her crippled husband's life. With that assurance she seemed content. She had already survived for much longer than I had expected. Her pain was under good control. Her ability to cook and clean was apparently unimpaired. Her will to live, her belief that she would be able to care for her husband until he died, were paramount factors in her home.

At that time of my life I had little experience of the way in which patients can deceive their doctors and themselves about their capacity for independent living. Later, I was to see and appreciate the efforts patients sometimes put into 'keeping up appearances'. They get up at 5.00 a.m. because they know it will take them several hours to get dressed in slow stages. Once dressed, 'facing the world' may well entail sitting in a chair or lying on their bed until the doorbell rings later in the morning, but, when it does, they will greet the visitor with smiles and 'small talk' that conceal pain, discomfort and even breathlessness, though that is a harder symptom to hide. After all, they think, the visitor, district nurse, postman, doctor, or member of the clergy will only be there for a limited period of time and, after that, they can return to being 'normal'.

Eva was one such patient. Those who cared for her professionally were never allowed to see her suffering. Her interests lay in her husband's health. She diverted her visitor's attention from herself.

As time went on, however, her pain was etched on her face. Her body wasted. Her husband, whom she never left alone with her doctors and nurses, looked unkempt and was found to have two bedsores on his buttocks, something from which he had never before suffered.

Although Eva was still on her feet, still immaculately dressed, still protesting she 'could manage', the time came when I had to tell her the truth. 'Harry needs a bit of treatment for his sores,' I said. 'And you need to get that pain under control.'

She smiled and accepted the half-truth. 'The time has come,' she said. 'I'm ready.'

We saw Harry off to his section of the hospital. When the ambulance came for her she was able to step into it with help.

Eva died on the way to hospital. She had not appeared to be in a terminal state even half-an-hour before her death. I think she knew, though, that her life was over. She had stopped hoping that she could go on. She had stopped believing that she would outlive her husband. She had faith in me. She trusted me to give her a signal when her time was up, and I had done that, as both of us knew. She quietly gave up the struggle and died peacefully and without the dreaded residence in a hospital bed for the terminally ill.

As a medical doctor, I have seen in many people this kind of faith response involving a strong desire to live until the completion of a self-determined task. An old person may long to see a beloved child who lives overseas. Such a person may well 'hang on' until the child can reach him or her. Once that task has been accomplished, death may come quite swiftly. My own aunt was like that. Her daughter lived in Australia. She longed to see her. The daughter and her son-in-law came for a holiday visit. They spent a happy three weeks together. By the time they left, the house was spotlessly clean, the garden tidied, stores laid in for the coming winter. It was the happiest possible time. There was no suggestion of imminent death. Two days after the young people had left, my aunt had a heart attack. She lived long enough for me to visit her in hospital. That was all.

Faith that encompasses both hope and the belief that one will accomplish the task one has set oneself is an important ingredient in people's lives, whether or not they possess religious faith.

Religious faith as a help to survival

Religious faith, faith in the existence of God, is, I believe, part of what it means to be human, but it is a dimension of life of which some people become conscious while others remain unaware of or impervious to it.

Scientists tell us that there is an area of the brain, which, if stimulated by electrodes, produces 'religious' experiences. One author, discussing this fact, adds that it would be natural for God, if God exists, to select a part of the brain that is capable of receiving messages from the supernatural world. The fact that faith is mediated by a finite part of the human brain does not necessarily mean that God does not exist.[4]

Religious faith is a factor in survival. That is undoubted. Where it comes from is another matter. Many people feel that religious faith is a set of responses that is implanted in childhood by the child's response to the presence, or absence, of parental love. If children experience the reality of unconditional love at the hands of their parents they can make the transition in their minds to belief in a God who loves them and the whole world. They have experience to build upon. Parents, however, may love their children wholeheartedly, yet their love may manifest itself predominantly in anxiety or criticism. If that happens, the children may not feel loved unconditionally. The parents' love is real enough but they have not found an adequate way of expressing it. Children may then feel that they can only be loved if they behave in ways that earn their parents' approval. That attitude, too, will transfer itself to their relationships with God, the supreme 'parent in the sky'. Happy are the children who experience unconditional love from a figure other than a parent in their early years. They can easily equate God's love with the unconditional love of the substitute parent.

That is why grandparents, aunts and uncles, and godparents are so important in children's lives. It is easier for them to give such love. They are not faced with the all-important task of rearing the children to be social adults.

As a child, I knew this unconditional love primarily through my mother's older sister, Nellie. She was the one who, when my mother was desperately unhappy after the breakdown of her marriage, took me into her bed in Libau, Latvia, on the first visit we made to that house. Hers was the fat warm body to which I could snuggle up at night and feel safe.

About a year later, when I was about four years old, I had my first religious experience in a totally different setting. It happened on a rare visit to my father's mother who lived in North London.

Granny Hill was a small, chubby, woman with a huge pile of white hair perched high on her head. It was surmounted by a black velvet ribbon which held the topknot in position. She had tiny hands, which she held on her lap with one hand scratching the back of the other in a kind of perpetual motion. I had been told that Granny Hill suffered from 'nerves' and I was reminded that small children must be very good and quiet so as not to upset her. My aunt must have had something else to do that day, for, almost as soon as we had arrived, she departed, saying that she would return during the afternoon.

I found myself alone with this rather formidable-looking old lady, who sat silently in a red velvet chair, the back of which was draped with a white lace antimacassar. I gravely accepted a biscuit and a cup of milk and sat down by her side. For a long time, or so it seemed to me, she said nothing at all. There was just the sound of her hand scratching at a red raw scab on the back of her wrist. Finally, she asked me if I would like to go for a walk. Anything seemed better than what we were doing, so I readily agreed.

'We'll go and see grandfather's gates,' she said. It turned out that those gates were to be found inside a church. I suppose that they must have been memorial gates, erected by his family in memory of his long years of merchant life in Russia. From this distance of time it is impossible to recall how large that church was. To a child, all size is relative. Inside, it was rather dark, but a dimly-coloured light slanted across the solid pews. Granny Hill took me down a long aisle opposite the door by which we had entered, towards the gates. We stood and stared. They were black wrought-iron gates, surmounted by some intricate gold scrolling. My grandmother had brought some flowers for the church. 'I'll go and put them in a vase,' she said. 'Just stay here by the gates and don't move till I come back.'

I peered through the gates Beyond them there was darkness but, off to the right, there was a tiny glimmering light. It's glow made me feel warm inside. It was a warmth evocative of the time I had woken up beside my Aunt Nellie in Latvia and found the cat at my feet. It was a safe, secure, happy sort of a feeling. When my grandmother returned, I did not want to go home, but that was not anything that a grown-up could possibly understand. She wanted a cup of tea, so she hustled me out of that church, out into the windy street and off as quickly as we could go towards the antimacassars, the china teapot and the dark, thick, milky tea which I disliked. It was small recompense for leaving that warm place inside the church.

It was, I think, my first experience of God. Of course, I knew nothing at all about such a Being. If anyone had asked me about it at the time, I would have said that my Aunt Nellie was in that church. The fact that, by this time in her life, Aunt Nellie was a confirmed atheist was quite immaterial. Later, much later, after I experienced this feeling again, I identified it as the experience of being loved, but I couldn't have told anyone that then. I have often wondered why I hadn't associated the warmth in that church with my mother. I think it is because her love for me, real as it was, was always mixed up with anxiety, either about me or about herself, and that anxiety clouded my ability to perceive her love. My Aunt Nellie's attitude towards me was that of a pure, unadulterated, enveloping kind of unselfish love, which came across very clearly.

I said nothing about this experience to anyone until long after I had become a Christian, but I never forgot it; to this day it is vivid in my memory. The memory of this experience has been a source of strength at various times of deep unhappiness in my life, for at such times I have been able to grope through the misery towards the warmth at the centre of my being.

That childhood experience of love was transferred to the concept of God without difficulty, but the other childhood experiences of pain at the hands of a man made it difficult for me to relate to Christ, the God-man whom I was encouraged to love and follow when I became a practising Christian. This difficulty is not unusual in children who have experienced suffering in early childhood. Yet, it has to be said that some children who are terribly abused in their early years can still find faith in God through Christ as an 'other', someone totally different from anyone they have ever experienced in their lives. They may be projecting an 'ideal' on to a concept; nevertheless, God becomes a reality in their lives and a potent ally in survival.

I count myself fortunate to have experienced both unconditional love and rejection and pain in childhood. Each of those experiences contributed to the development of religious faith in me. They were to sustain me through many years of rejection at the hands of the institutional Anglican Church. I had come to God by both routes. Later doubts, difficulties and hardships in life were unable to budge me from a fundamental belief in the existence of Love, an unconditional acceptance that could sometimes be found in people and always in God.

These developmental components of religious faith are important in understanding the role of religious faith in survival after disaster. People often lose their faith at such a time. God has not given them what they prayed for. They feel abandoned, rejected, cruelly treated. Their anger with God, whom they think of as an all-powerful controller can, of course, become a means of sustaining them through the crisis. Loss of religious faith becomes part of survival. Professional Christians, like myself, may find this difficult, but it is possible to see the loss of faith as a God-given contributory factor to immediate survival. Faith may return after the initial period of anger is over, and its return may be facilitated by sensitive pastoral care during the time when faith is lost.

I have personally found Psalm 139 a great help to my own faith when I see friends and parishioners struggling with God after being hit by some terrible disaster. In verse 11 we read, 'even the darkness is not dark to you; the night is as bright as the day, for darkness is as light to you'.[5] These words remind me that God is present everywhere, that Jesus can descend even into hell, and that nothing is alien to love of that kind, not even faithlessness. And I always tell people who cannot pray when they are ill or hit by tragedy or catastrophe of any kind, that their job is to survive. My task, and that of their friends, at such a time, is to go on believing and praying, even when they cannot. I do not necessarily spell out that fact in bold words, but I do try to communicate it in non-verbal ways. It is sometimes a comfort to non-believers to be accompanied by those who can still believe, provided that faith is not applied to them like a plaster bandage. Nothing can assuage the pain of their own experience. Religious faith is neither a placebo nor bandage to hide suffering from view.

Being needed as a help to survival

Some time ago, I sat in the small tidy room of an old man whom I had visited a long time previously when I was his family doctor. His wife had died from a massive haemorrhage after the birth of their youngest child. After Mary's death, I had visited him quite often because he was so smitten with grief that I had been worried about the possibility of suicidal ruminations. I had never uncovered any. Relatives and friends urged him to allow the children, a little girl aged two and a newborn boy, to be adopted or fostered by 'a good woman'. In those days, all foster mothers still had a good image.

'No', he said. 'No, I'll bring them up on my own.'

Despite heavy pressure and appeals to him 'to do the manly thing' and go back to his well-paid full-time work to provide financially for his children, he left work. He lived on the then meagre provisions of social security, and raised his children.

At the time of my visit, he was plainly moving towards the end of his life.

'Tom', I said, 'Are you glad you did what you did?'

'Yes,' he answered firmly. 'You see, what I never told you at the time was that six weeks after Mary died, I was ready to give up altogether. My sister came in one day to look after the children to give me a break. The little one had been fretful for a few days and I hadn't had much sleep. That morning, I took our car and drove as fast as I could to the South Coast, to Beachy Head. I meant to drive the car straight over the cliffs. I got within yards of the cliff and got out for one last look at the beauty of the world. The children were too little to miss me, I thought. My sister would probably rear them with her own family. It would be better for them. So I got back in the car and started the engine. Quick as a flash, the thought came into my head that they would never know either their mother or their father except through some old black and white pictures. "Not even in colour," I shouted angrily. I reversed the car and drove back to London. You came in the next morning, bright as a button, and I raged at you for letting Mary die. You never answered me a word, but sat down quite still until I'd finished. Then you kissed me, and asked if you might look at our little son. You never knew, did you?'

'No,' I said, 'I never knew.'

'That day was the turning point for me,' Tom went on, 'but I needed to be with the children all the time to remind myself that they needed me. I thought I ought to tell you that before I die.'

'Thank you,' I said, and we turned to the tea he had laid out so carefully on the table and enjoyed the rest of our time together.

Many people survive bereavement and other disasters simply because they are reminded of the needs of their children, or dogs, or even their budgerigar. Some, of course, do not. Life as a survivor simply seems too awful to contemplate. Time and again, though, I have seen men and women live through experiences, and do things that seem beyond reason, simply because they have dependants. Their love for those who have need of them keeps them going.

One of the best times of my life, though I did not know it at the time, came to me when I had to leave general practice and move into community medicine as a school doctor. I took this course of action so that I could avoid night-work and care more adequately for my husband.

Initially, I hated the work. School doctors could not prescribe medicines, had little real responsibility and were at the bottom of the profession. I had been used to a good deal of responsibility and I did not see that what I was doing had any real value. How wrong I was.

Part of my work as a community school doctor was to assess physically and mentally handicapped children. We looked at their needs and then fought to supply them out of the small resources at our disposal. We tried to ensure that they got the kind of education and care that they needed. It was then, over a period of some seven years, that I met some heroic parents who were the scourge of the health and education services. Their love for their wholly dependent children not only led them to care for them day and night, year after year; it also led them to try to secure the best care and education available. Frustration often led to anger, and anger is an uncomfortable emotion when you are on the receiving end and can do very little to assuage it.

Meeting these 'difficult', often belligerent, relatives gave me insight into the value of their being needed, not only by their sick and handicapped children, but also by society as a whole. During those seven years, and frequently since, I have seen major changes in the schooling and community care of children with special needs. Those changes would not have come about if some parents had not raised the consciousness of the professionals, and if some professionals had not understood the parents' concern that lay behind awkward behaviour. More physically disabled children now enjoy integrated schooling. More intellectually impaired children now get the education they deserve, so that they can take part in successful independent life when they leave school. There is still a long way to go, but a good beginning has been made.

Being needed is undoubtedly a spur to successful survival. Yet the aim should always be to achieve the maximum possible independence for those who are dependent on the help of others if they are to live at all.

Work as a spur to survival

Faith and being needed have priority in my list of factors that help people to survive disaster. I am in two minds about the relative importance of work and friendship as aids to successful survival. In the end, I put work first because it has been work, rather than friendships, that has so often kept me going, but in reality both, I think, are of equal value to survivors.

Work, particularly paid work, is of great value to someone who has to struggle to regain self-esteem after a disaster such as forced redundancy, divorce, disablement or bereavement. Many people, finding their lives turned upside-down by disaster, are able to cling to work as a means of earning a living. It is something they feel they have to do. It is an anodyne against too much thought about their personal situation. Work 'takes them out of themselves'. It lends some sort of stability to each day. It can also be used as a way of making oneself so tired that one can go to sleep. I have already mentioned the widow who worked by night during the early years of her widowhood because she could not sleep. In my own case, I worked so hard physically during the first two years of widowhood that I exhausted other people by my energy. That energy was forced. I was driven to work by the need to survive, and I worked far too hard and with far too little sleep for my own good during those years.

The aftermath of disaster, however, can be so dreadful that a person's ability to hold down a job may be impaired. Time and again, I have seen people lose their jobs after a partner has left them. I have listened to men who have been made redundant at the age of fifty telling me that their initial determination to secure another job was destroyed by repeated rejection. In the end, long-term unemployment has not only embittered them, it has eroded their self-esteem. It has left them as 'burnt-out' people. Some people who have fallen off the ladder of success can only think of themselves as failures. That failure has reinforced their sense of inadequacy in social interaction; they have slowly become isolated from friends and more affluent relatives.

Society recognizes that work is important in the rehabilitation of people but it provides relatively little help to those who become dispirited through loss of work, loss of status and loss of economic stability. So long as a social value system is based upon one's position in the 'pecking order' and one's ability to achieve economic success, this harmful effect of losing work is inevitable.

Those of us who are close to people who lose their self-esteem have to try to reverse these harsh effects of our social structure by a ministry of encouragement. The capacity of people to adapt to changed circumstances is immense, if only it can be tapped. I have seen some men who were once highly paid executives managing to redeploy their skills in other ways. I have seen other men overcome the change in their economic status through adapting to their new circumstances: they move into wholly new fields of work and become content with a different lifestyle. I have seen widows grit their teeth and take low-paid jobs for the first time in their lives so that they can support their family. I have also seen men and women sacrificing their work in order to care for a dependent relative.

The principal factor that enables people to survive such economic and emotional disasters lies in their ability to assign value to themselves as human beings, quite apart from the status given to them by society. Worth should not depend on work. Once people can be helped to understand that their intrinsic worth is not necessarily related to their extrinsic position in society they can begin to regain self-esteem, discover hidden talents and even recover their happiness, or discover an entirely new way of being fulfilled in life.

The reasons for people being able to separate self-esteem from economic success are complex. Conversations with those who know how to give encouragement have been most helpful to me personally. I have needed such help quite often in my life.

During a long career I have both been dismissed from work I loved and resigned from work I detested. I have progressively gone down in the world so far as my professional status is concerned, because each time I have lost or given up a job and secured a new one I have had to start again from the beginning, to earn my way up to parity, so to speak. When my husband became ill and I had to give up a very pleasant life as a family doctor for a job as a school doctor, our income was halved. My status in the profession fell. Our lifestyle changed greatly. When my husband died and I retired early from paid work, I found myself living on a relatively modest pension. I could have supplemented that income by again taking up paid work as a doctor, but I chose not to. Instead I sought to do voluntary work for the church.

Now that I am old, in a young-hearted kind of a way, I have realized that the reason work has been so important to me is that it has given external structure to my life. Although paid employment was useful in economic ways, before reaching retirement I spent seven years in all working only for my keep, nearly five of those as a nun and two as an overseas missionary. Throughout that time, I enjoyed a balanced life of prayer, work, rest and sleep. Work was varied and productive, stimulating and interesting, and the fact that it was there to be done each day lent balance to my life. That is not to say that the work itself was always pleasurable or satisfying. Often it was not. Much of my life as a junior nun was spent doing housework, cleaning the church brass and participating in things I did not enjoy at all. Yet the external structure of each day, its very monotony, provided a framework within which my interior life could be set free to flourish. In that respect I have been singularly fortunate, for I am blessed with a rich and creative imagination and it serves me well during long periods when I have been physically engaged in routine work.

The rhythm of work during each day, whether imposed by external employment, or determined by my own internal needs, has given stability to my life. It has often given me pleasure. During my years as a widow it has warded off depression and prevented me from becoming a recluse. It has given me a sense of fulfilment. Now that I am able to choose when to work and when to rest, it has provided me with a measure of freedom to enjoy leisure to the full. Work has also provided me with the incentive to keep well informed concerning issues that I care about, and to remain engaged in those interests despite my growing physical disabilities. Like many other people for whom work is important during their active years of retirement, I enjoy what I do and intend to go on doing it as long as I can do the work effectively. Then I shall stop.

I anticipate that when I can no longer work I shall still enjoy life. The external rhythm will be different, but I have complemented active work by spending hours of my life learning to enjoy doing nothing except being who I am. It is as if I am a piece of parched dry land waiting for rain to fall. I am thirsty but content to wait for the rain to come. When it comes, as it sometimes does, I am happy and the flowers blossom, so to speak, but I know that the dry times will come and I also know that I will survive them because I have past experience upon which to build.

The blessing of friendship

I think I know what friendship is all about, yet, when I come to write about it, I find it hard to define. For me, friendship is a bond between people who maintain their individual lifestyles. It involves intimacy, loyalty that goes beyond disagreement, a desire to maintain communication, even at a distance, concern and care that go beyond the ordinary, a sharing that goes deeper than words. Partners, indeed all blood relatives, can be friends with each other, but friendship does not necessarily mean the kind of intimacy in which boundaries between two people are dissolved so that they become one flesh.

Friendships are important to me. The only reason I have put work first in my list of factors that have helped me to survive disaster is that there was a time in my life when I found myself without certain valued friends. Work pulled me through that dreadful experience.

People like myself, people who try to change the structures of society, often make themselves unpopular by their words and actions. In my case, I and others were trying to bring about a change in the earning capacity of men and women in our society. We were also trying to urge society to provide women with equal opportunities to those of men. It was hard work. I spent nearly twelve years of my life, from 1967 to 1979, swimming against the stream of thought and practice that was prevalent in society. Because my work brought me to public notice, I also offended many people in the Church of England, to which I was passionately committed. So I attracted strong criticism for some of my actions. At times, I found myself ostracized by people whom I admired. I was quite able to withstand criticism from my opponents. I did not do nearly so well when I found myself losing friends whose aims and objectives were the same as my own, but whose methods were different, and who condemned me for my behaviour as a result.

It is said that disaster sorts out one's real friends from one's supposed friends. During that decade of difficulty in my life, I remember something that happened to a friend of mine that helped me to come to terms with losing those whom I had previously thought to be good friends.

One day, a day when I was feeling particularly low because of an unpleasant letter from someone I had once trusted implicitly, the phone rang. The priest on the other end of the line told me that he had just come out of prison. I had always respected this man. Indeed, I had trusted him with my own problems at one time. I had never had the slightest suspicion of his tendency to criminal behaviour. I wanted to tell him I would have nothing to do with him. Yet, at that moment, I recalled my own feelings when someone I valued and trusted had rejected me because I had done something that was unacceptable. I had barely survived the loss of that friend. The man on the other end of the phone deserved better than that from me. So I invited him to a meal.

The rest of the story about his relationship and mine is immaterial, except to say that we remain friends although we live far from one another and seldom meet. I had come so close to rejecting him, because I disapproved of his behaviour, that I gained insight into people who had rejected me. I had felt, as others had felt about me, that if I continued to associate with him I would be guilty of tacit approval of his actions. I had felt he was harming people, just as others had felt that I was harming the church I loved by my campaigns. This insight gave me some understanding of the people who could not, in conscience, associate with me. It also gave me insight into the possible consequences of friendship.

Friendship is sealed by loyalty in disaster. That loyalty may, and often does, tarnish one's own reputation. Standing by a friend in trouble does not necessarily imply that one supports that person's actions, but it is often taken to mean that one is condoning behaviour that is unacceptable to other people. Friends, true friends, have to be prepared to be 'tarred with the same brush'. They have to be prepared, if necessary, to lose others they counted as friends. They may, in consequence, become defensive in ways that are quite offensive to others, belligerent towards others who are hostile to them. That is one of the consequences of friendship; loyalty can distort character. Yet it need not do so.

The intimacy of friendship makes a person privy to other people's secrets. The more one knows about another person, the more vulnerable he or she becomes to the possibility that the confidant(e) may abuse that secret knowledge. Such betrayal by a friend is well illustrated in the Bible by the story of Jesus and his friends, Judas and Peter, as found in Luke chapter 22.

Judas betrayed Jesus with a kiss. He could not live with himself once he realized what he had done and so he killed himself. Peter did not betray Jesus in quite the same way. He merely denied that he knew him in order to save his own skin. He, too, was overcome with shame at his threefold action, yet he survived. We do not know why Judas killed himself and Peter decided to go on living, but I personally think that, when Jesus looked at Peter after this threefold denial, Peter perceived that Jesus forgave him and still loved him. Judas seemingly never had that opportunity, at least he never did during his lifetime, though, again, my personal opinion is that he ultimately knew he was forgiven and loved.

In my own life there have been many occasions when I could have betrayed friends by disclosing knowledge I have about their lives. A strong professional ethic has prevented me from that kind of action, but that does not mean to say that I have not at times wanted to 'get my own back' at them when they have hurt, betrayed or rejected me. Now that I am old I can admit to those feelings, but I also know that the strongest ethic in my whole life has been that of not doing to others what they do to me. I will not pay back in kind.

I do not stand on any high moral ground in this ethic. I simply realize that, should I compromise, then, like Judas, I will end up destroying myself. It is I who will be diminished by my action, not my close friend. I also realize that repayment of hurt for hurt, revenge for revenge, will not help my friend, but merely perpetuate the vendetta. It was not the way of Christ and, although I am a poor disciple, I want to follow his way, not the way of nature.

Although I have not, in the main, been susceptible to betraying my friends, I have been vulnerable to their rejection shown through their disapproval of my actions. When people have broken off friendships or withdrawn their trust from me, I have found it incredibly difficult not to become destroyed by their action. My self-esteem plummets when erstwhile friends stop communicating with me. My desire never to risk another encounter with them, or indeed with anyone else, increases. Becoming a recluse may initially protect me from further hurt, but it does nothing to heal me. My pride in being a good friend to others is wounded and I risk becoming embittered by my failure to recover from such disappointments.

Such reactions to the loss of friendship can easily lead to a person becoming lost in self-justification. That leads to a defensive hardness of heart and ultimately to self-pity. By the grace of God, I have not developed a thick skin. Although sadness at what has happened to some of my friendships as a result of my actions has persisted, I am fierce with myself at the first signs of self-pity. I do not want to wallow in sorrow. I do not want to become isolated and reclusive because I am afraid of trying to form new relationships.

What has saved me in such situations has been work, hard work, and more hard work, coupled with the fact that I believe, though I do not always remember it, that I am cherished by God in the person of Jesus.

The loss of friends who have formerly confided their inmost secrets to me, and now wish to keep their distance for fear of being reminded of those secrets, is not so distressing because it is much more understandable. It does not imply that they disapprove of me to the point of rejection. It still hurts, but it is part of the life of any confidante or confessor. If someone has spent a lot of time telling me about secrets, the last thing that seems desirable to them, if and when they manage to mend a broken relationship, is to be reminded of that crisis in their life. Better to make a break and start anew. I miss these friends but their absence does not make the same impact on my self-esteem and confidence as the kind of rejection I have formerly described.

I have outlined some of the difficulties of friendship because they are not always obvious at the outset of a friendly relationship. To give oneself in friendship is to take the risk of being hurt. A broken friendship can greatly impair one's chances of survival. All these dangers are magnified a thousandfold when the friendship matures into a partnership that is more than a sexual relationship and that involves the day-to-day intimacy of shared life. That is why divorce can be so devastating to one or both partners.

On the other hand, some friendships have been most helpful to me. They have kept me alive and also helped me to mature as a person. I have cherished those friends, particularly some of my companions on the Christian journey, and I owe them a great deal. My husband was my greatest friend in life. Since he died, I have discovered great joy in the sustained friendships that continue, some of which extend back to childhood, some of which are relatively new. My friends' faith in me, in my ability to survive the rejections and reverses of life, have done more to sustain my hope than I can easily describe. I am grateful for the gift of close and loyal personal friends.

Asked, as I often am, if I feel that Jesus is my friend, I reply, 'Yes', but I also echo St Theresa of Avila's famous riposte. This fifteenth-century Spanish saint was a tireless worker on Christ's behalf. She helped to reform the Carmelite order to which she belonged. She urged the primacy of prayer on her nuns. She founded many reformed convents. She laboured to bring in Christ's kingdom. She met with opposition from important and influential people in the church. She lost friends and patrons. She was suspected by many of being a hysteric and false mystic. Once, when crossing a turbulent river in appalling weather, she nearly drowned. She metaphorically shook her fists at God and said, 'If this is how you treat your friends, dear God, no wonder you have so few.'[6] Sometimes that is how I feel as well, and yet I would say that God is my friend.

Moments of enlightenment

Moments of enlightenment are the sudden insights that come from outside one's immediate self, thought or experience. They come because 'no [one] is an island, entire unto itself'.[7] We who are human gain immense riches from the communities to which we belong.

Sudden moments of illumination or insight can come from anyone at any time. A mother going shopping with her two-year-old son may suddenly be struck by an advertisement about the plight of children in the Third World. Before she saw that poster, she was unaware of, maybe indifferent to, the fact that many children in the impoverished debt-ridden countries of our world die before they reach the age of two. After seeing the poster she may find herself moved by compassion to try and do something about those children in whatever small way she can. A person watching a TV 'soap' may suddenly gain insight into a dilemma in their own relationships. A phrase in a book may unexpectedly move a reader to tears. In as much as we are surrounded by people who are constantly trying to communicate with each other, we are subject to other people's thoughts all the time. Such outside thoughts may reverberate with unspoken, hitherto unknown, feelings in someone who is desperate to survive but who feels that he or she is 'going under', drowning in an unfriendly and hostile environment, or overwhelmed by grief and/or guilt.

In our twenty-first-century world we are bombarded by thoughts through the media. It is difficult to be selective about those images that are projected on to our brains, whether or not we want them to be. I seldom try to stop them. It is always possible that one or other phrase, sound-bite or visual image may help me to survive the next hour, the next day, the next week. What I try to do, however, is to sift those outside thoughts and images in silence. I reckon that things which are important to me will be recalled, while things that are unimportant will remain buried deep in my memory and only surface when I need them.

Some years ago I experienced a profound feeling of disappointment when a colleague told me that she did not trust me, indeed, had never trusted me. My sense of hurt and rejection persisted for a good part of the day. Then, quite unasked, some words that I had read many years before came back to haunt me.

Shortly after my husband died I had visited the Holy Land. On one of my days there, the party I was with had been taken to the top of a hill which had been designated as the site of the transfiguration of Jesus. The hill where this really occurred was probably some distance away from this one, but the event of the transfiguration is so deeply embedded in Christian consciousness that access to a symbolic site where pilgrims can meditate on it has been important to the many generations of people who have visited it.

At the top of the hill there is a chapel dug out of the rock. While we were there, the Eucharist was being celebrated. I sat on the steps outside the chapel. I could not get my mind to focus on the service. I was still deeply bereaved and restless. So I got up and wandered around outside. One plaque caught my eye; one only. On it were inscribed these words: 'The road to glory passes through the valley of humiliation.' They had, I think, been put there by the Sisters of Mary, a Protestant religious order from Darmstadt in Germany. The founder of the order, Basilea Schlink, certainly knew what humiliation and vilification were like, for she had endured plenty of both during the foundation years of her order, and those words came straight from her heart.[8] They were apt, because, after the time on the mountaintop, Jesus and his three friends, Peter, James and John, had gone down into the valley. There, Jesus had gone from the ecstasy of transfiguration and rich blessing to his capture, humiliation, torture and death at the hands of his enemies and former friends. In their several ways, his friends had to endure their own humiliation because they abandoned their friend in his greatest hour of need. Those events were recorded for all to read, but the ending of the story is a happy one, for after the cross had been endured 'for the sake of the joy that was set before him' (Hebrews 12:2), glory was restored to Jesus.

As I read those words on the Mount of Transfiguration I felt profoundly moved. They told me not only about Jesus, but about the disciples who had, through many centuries, shared his experience in their unique but different ways. My own humiliation, on the day that I saw those words, was that I was unable to feel any stirring of faith in that place. I was locked into scepticism. In a curious way I found the words a comfort, the source of a flicker of hope that I might, at some time in the future, again know the glory of belief. It seems to me that, whether or not one believes in God or the divinity of Christ, these great stories in the Bible speak of and to the human condition.

We came back from our pilgrimage to our own country. Shortly afterwards, I left my childhood home for ever and embarked on a new phase of my journey through life. I forgot the words for many years. They must, however, have been deeply embedded in my subconscious mind for, when I needed them, they came back to the surface. They provided me with the strength to continue my relationship with my colleague, while knowing for certain that she was highly critical of my work. They continued to reverberate in my mind for many days.

The words, however, did more than simply sustain me. They gave me insight. At the time of my husband's prolonged illness and death, I had found it difficult to remain faithful and trusting in God. My colleague's lack of trust in me was only an echo of my former lack of trust in the existence of God. If God could put up with my mean attitude, then I could put up with my colleague's suspicion of me. I laughed out aloud and got on with the next task in hand.

Moments of illumination, such as I have described, can come at any time, at any place and through any source. Survivors are highly sensitive to spoken and unspoken communication in the weeks, months and, sometimes, years following a major disaster. Those who are close to them have a responsibility to provide them with words of encouragement and hope, rather than of criticism. Silent support is better still, for it allows the person's past memories to surface uncluttered by superficial chatter. People who are survivors of disaster need time and space to recover, and they need to recover in their own way, I would say with the help of God, the Holy Spirit, who implants these ideas into our consciousness when we most need them.

It seems to me that these helpful factors that I have described – faith in its broadest sense, religious faith, the needs of dependants, work, friendships and moments of illumination – are positive factors in enabling people to survive disaster or the deep natural traumas of life. Analysis, and even good therapeutic application, of these principles, cannot, however, fully explain the mystery of survival. In my professional life, both as a doctor and as a Christian minister, I have seen people in whom all these factors were present, but who, nevertheless, have decided that life is not worth living. They have killed themselves, often in bizarre ways that inflict punishment on themselves and on their surviving relatives. I have been alongside people in whom none of the external factors that help people to survive are present, but who have doggedly gone on living through sheer anger at their circumstances.

While I cannot correctly predict who will go under and who will survive, I can, at least, discern signs that indicate someone may be moving from sheer survival to a fresh start in his or her life. Those signs will engage me in the next chapter.

6

Getting stuck

'After we had reached safety, we then learned that the island was called
Malta. The natives showed us unusual kindness.'
(Acts 28:1–2a)

When St Paul was a prisoner on his way to Rome, the ship that was
carrying him and other prisoners was caught in a great storm and
shipwrecked. Some of the soldiers guarding Paul wanted to kill him
and his fellow prisoners, but the centurion in charge of them wanted
to spare Paul and so he 'kept them from carrying out their plan' (Acts
27:43). When they had all landed safely, they met with 'unusual
kindness' and the whole party stayed on the island for three months.

We know from Luke's account in the Acts of the Apostles that the
centurion went on to do his duty. After a period of respite, the
centurion, the guards, Paul and the other prisoners moved on towards
their destiny in Rome. Many of us, who perhaps have more control
over our lives than Paul had over his, find that we do not move on
from the plateau we reach when we have survived disaster. We may
look normal, behave appropriately, seem happy to outsiders and yet
be stuck in a relatively successful survival mode, being unable to move
on from sheer survival to a new beginning.

This condition is well known to many survivors, but few like to
talk about it. Before I move on to a fuller discussion of the ways in
which people can know when they are ready to do more than just
survive, ready to make a fresh start, I need to outline some of the
subtle ways in which people can get stuck at the level of survival.

Difficulties related to major shifts in social and religious attitudes

I can best describe this difficulty by referring to a time when I got stuck in this way. It happened within the last decade of the twentieth century. By this time, I had been aware of an internal desire to become an Anglican priest for over fifty years. In the early years of this interior prompting I had kept very quiet about it. I treated it as a fantasy, an unachievable goal. In my youth I diverted its dynamism into life as a missionary nun-doctor. When that venture came to an end, I used my frustrated energy as a mother and general practitioner. It was only when the idea surfaced at the Lambeth Conference of 1968 that there were no theological reasons to prevent women from becoming Anglican priests that I began to hope that my calling might be fulfilled.

I was in for a long wait. Twenty-five years were to pass before the General Synod of the Church of England agreed that such a calling might be from God and could be tested in the ordinary way. By that time I had left England and was resident in Wales. I watched the events from afar. In November 1992 General Synod voted to allow English women to become priests.

Like many of my friends, I was elated at the result and subsequently downcast by the Act of Synod brought in by the bishops of the Church of England to provide 'flying bishops' for those who could not accept the decision of General Synod. Compromise is necessary at times, but we foresaw that this compromise was one of principle and it would have wider implications for the church than the bishops seemed aware of at the time.

Events have proved us right. Once the diocesan bishop ceased to be a focus of unity, a person who held together people of widely differing views, the way was open for anarchy. Now, at the beginning of the twenty-first century, any Anglican who does not like the views of his or her bishop can challenge his authority. Parishes can decide to flout the authority of their own diocesan bishop in favour of someone who complies with their idea of what is right. Already, scarcely five years after the Act of Synod passed into law, clergy who dislike their diocesan bishop's views on homosexuality can prevent him from visiting their parish for confirmations.[1] The matter will not stop there: if fragmentation of authority is possible over a few issues, it will eventually develop over many areas of controversy.

The Church of England is not alone in its dilemma over authority. The more hierarchical an organization, the more vulnerable it is to such challenges. When, for instance, Archbishop Lefebvre, of the Roman Catholic Church, disagreed with Pope Paul VI over the implementation of the principles agreed at Vatican II, he simply refused to accept the conciliar reforms and went on his own way, ordaining men to the priesthood without reference to the generally accepted practices of the mainstream Roman Catholic communion.[2]

These notable instances of the breakdown in hierachical authority simply reflect a more general change in attitudes towards designated authority of all kinds. The Roman Catholic Church has been unable to get all its members to accept *Humanae Vitae*.[3] These changes in people's attitudes towards statements that issue from those in the church who hold designated authority simply reflect a more widespread attitude towards authority in general. Statements made by governments, and by governing bodies of professions such as medicine and the law, are regularly challenged. Authority now has to be earned, not conferred. It has to be consonant with knowledge and practice, not automatically obeyed simply because it is held by those in powerful positions in society.

This paradigm shift in social attitudes towards authority – from designated authority to consensus authority – is like an earthquake in its effects on people who have to live through the period of instability that follows such a shift. It leaves individuals like myself bewildered and uncertain about its consequences in our small lives. If, like me, you have spent a good part of your life listening to people who hold designated authority and following their precepts, you do not find it at all easy to change. You feel uncomfortable about relying solely on an informed individual conscience as a guide to your behaviour in society.

It was the difficulty of making this paradigm shift in the nature of authority that was seriously to undermine my own ability to move from successful survival to a new beginning in life, but I only discovered this after I had become a priest, not before.

The first women priests in the Church of England were ordained in the Bristol diocese on the 15 March 1993. Just over a year later, the Governing Body of the Church in Wales voted negatively on the ordination of women.[4] Women in Wales were left behind. For me, it was a personal disaster, but it was not unexpected. Being used to accepting the decisions of representative bodies such as the Governing

Body of the Church of England and the Church in Wales, I accepted the decision. It came, however, at an awkward time in my own personal journey.

Between April 1994 and December 1994 there were several options still open to me. By the time of the Welsh refusal to ordain women to the priesthood, I had moved from Tymawr convent to a small house in Monmouth. I was having a trial year as a 'solitary' but I had not yet made life vows of stability and conversion of manners. During those six months I could, for instance, have still gone back to the convent and returned to my life as a contemplative nun. I could have abandoned my solitary way of life and gone to England, both to be nearer to my children and to seek to fulfil my calling as an Anglican priest. I could have continued to be a solitary, going against the mainstream life of my cherished religious order and continuing as a deacon in the Church in Wales. Matters were complicated by my age. In April 1994 I was sixty-eight years old. By the time of the next possible vote I would be over seventy years old, and would thus have reached the age of compulsory retirement for clergy in Wales. Furthermore, I was suffering from serious health problems, problems which were exacerbated by an internal conflict about the right course of action to take.

In the event I did what so many people who are accustomed to surviving successive disasters do. I settled for a pragmatic compromise; a course that fell short of what I really wanted to happen but that was 'good enough' given the circumstances. I did not believe I ought to go back to the convent. I was afraid of going to England in case I would be rejected. I was even more afraid of disconnecting myself entirely from the authority of the church to which I belonged. So I settled down to live a life of prayer and to be a deacon; as I thought, a permanent deacon.

I did not realize that I had got stuck. I thought I was being 'well adjusted' to a situation over which I had no personal control. I, and others, continued to work for the goals that we still shared, but hope – the personal hope that I might one day be able to become a priest – had flown away. Since then, I have often asked myself whether there was any flicker of hope left, and maybe at a subconscious level there was, but, if so, I was certainly not aware of it. The personal dynamism in me had been expunged.

The consequence was that I stopped growing. I had survived disappointment. It may have been a small disappointment compared to what other people have to suffer in their lives, but to me it was a massive reversal of fortune nonetheless. The effects of getting stuck were quick to appear. Indeed, for a time I appeared to be going backwards rather than to be stuck on a plateau from which there was no escape.

While I had still held out hope of reaching my goal, I had managed to overlook elements of resentment and bitterness that lurked deep down within me. Only a year earlier, I had been delighted to be present when the first of my English friends had been ordained in Bristol. Now, however, I found myself consumed with envy. In the months following the negative decision of the Church in Wales, I could scarcely bring myself to attend my English friends' ordinations or their first services as priests. I did not rejoice when I heard of the advancement of a woman in her career. I began to feel antagonistic again towards male clergy, especially those with whom I worked on a day-to-day basis.

I had thought that I had successfully managed my sense of frustration. It was a bitter blow to discover that my own reversal in fortune had uncovered negative feelings that were both unwanted and unwelcome, but which were apparently as strong as they had ever been. Acknowledgment of my state of mind, however, set me free. I stopped going backwards, regained the plateau I had occupied in my latter years, and remained there.

To all intents and purposes I looked well adjusted. I enjoyed my work as a deacon. I continued to support other women in the same situation. We even managed to laugh at the Church in Wales, and at ourselves, for the absurd situations we sometimes found ourselves in as a result of trying to do our work with 'one hand tied behind our backs'. Swapping stories with each other about the ridiculous lengths to which we had to go to obtain pre-consecrated bread and wine with which to feed our congregations during Sunday worship, sometimes obtaining this from elderly and indisposed male clergy, helped us to survive during the next three years. Sisterly compassion for one another helped to overcome our frustrations. For all that, I knew that I had stopped growing as a person. A vital spark in me had been extinguished. My apparent happiness was a delusion, a pretence.

At this point in my story I need to pause before I can go on to describe how I was ultimately able to move forward. I have given a detailed account of my success in reaching a plateau of survival. I have said that I could not move on from there. I had, however, up to this point, successfully ignored another factor that was operative. To illustrate this, I now need to turn to someone else who faced the same dilemma, but in whom the effects were more obvious and more easy to understand. I will call her Laura.

Fears concealed by rational arguments

Laura was a Christian who had strong views about her marriage vows. When she was married at the age of twenty, she had made those vows with sincerity. She had intended them to be for life. She thought that Tom, her husband, also a Christian, had made his vows in the same spirit.

Laura and Tom had three children. Laura was a realist. She had not expected marriage to be easy, so she was not unduly disappointed when difficulties of many different kinds surfaced in the years succeeding their wedding. She felt secure in her belief that her relationship with Tom would last until one of them died. It was, therefore, a considerable shock when Tom announced that he was leaving her for another woman; another Christian woman. One day the whole family was sitting round the table at suppertime; the next evening he was gone.

Laura had to survive for the sake of her stricken three children, all by then in their teens. Her friends rallied round. Some uttered platitudes. Some observed a sympathetic silence. One or two were disparaging about Tom: 'Good riddance, I say'; 'Hope he goes to hell'; 'Forget him: get yourself a decent husband.' Those kinds of sentiment may have been intended to express sympathy and outrage, but Laura was not yet ready for such expressions of anger. Her responses were swift, and, she believed, Christian. 'I forgive him, I'll take him back if he wants to come back,' she said. 'No, I'll never marry again. Marriage is for life.'

The vicar of the church to which Laura continued to go was a wise man. He said very little to her in the early stages of her separation, but he gave her support. During the next two years, Laura had a little desultory but amiable communication with Tom over the children's financial support. Laura was thankful that he was not an irresponsible father; she continued to maintain links with him about the children and encouraged them to see him. Once, when their telephone conversation seemed to be going well, she told Tom that she still loved him and missed him dreadfully. Tom did not reply directly, but he was friendly enough to rekindle some hope in Laura. They never talked about Sarah, the woman to whom he had gone when he had left her. Two years after he had left the marital home, Laura received a letter from him asking for a divorce.

Laura realized that Tom wanted to marry Sarah. For the first time in two years she felt angry with him. After a great deal of internal turmoil, and a series of consultations with her vicar, Laura decided to grant Tom his request. When the decree absolute came through, Laura put it in her desk drawer and tried to forget about it. She did not take off her wedding ring, as she still considered herself to be married to Tom.

A few months later, she found herself drawn into friendship with Francis, another member of the church. She told him firmly that she was unable to contemplate remarriage. 'I'm still married,' she said. 'I'm not expecting Tom to die, and while he's alive I can't remarry.'

The next few months were agonizing for them both. Laura had survived one break-up of marriage. Although she did not fully realize it at the time, she was also afraid of risking another permanent relationship. She remained stuck in survival mode and could not reach out to seize the happiness that her children and friends felt she deserved. Eventually, however, she compromised and agreed to sexual intimacy. A few months later, she set up home with Francis. At the same time, Laura stopped receiving Holy Communion.

Laura's attitude, according to her friends, might have been logical, and it obviously was to her, but it felt antiquated to many of them, especially when other people in her church had no such scruples. Laura, however, persisted. In her eyes, she was an adulteress, too sinful to remain a communicant member of the church. Yet she also knew that she was not as happy as she might have been. Francis had never been married. He wanted to marry her. She wanted to marry him and would have done so, she thought, had it not been for her belief in the indissolubility of marriage during the lifetime of a former partner.

Life continued in this manner for the next five years. Laura continued to live with Francis, but she was not quite the same vivacious person he had fallen in love with when they met. She was quieter, less prepared to go out with friends, less receptive to Francis' lovemaking, even occasionally making inadequate excuses to avoid intimacy. On one such occasion, Francis reproached her bitterly. 'If you really think we're "living in sin",' he said, 'you ought to leave me.' She, however, could not do that. They drifted on together.

Then Francis had a heart attack and died. Laura had retained her principles about marriage, but she had lost a precious opportunity for the kind of growth that is possible in the stable and open relationship of marriage. She never remarried.

It is a sad but true story. Laura's failure to do more than survive was not wholly a matter of principle. In her case, as I have already indicated, her principles partially concealed a deep-seated fear of the risk involved in remarriage. She could not, at the time, face that fear, so she pushed it well away from her with a rational argument. The argument had not prevented her from living with Francis, as it might have done had she carried it to its logical conclusion. If she had done this, then she might have looked again at her true beliefs about the indissolubility of marriage, and perhaps arrived at a different decision.

People like myself and Laura sometimes only find out what our true beliefs and principles are when we are challenged by other people and issues that affect us personally. Fears about what will happen if we dare to move on, if we seize our chance of happiness, are potent deterrents to our ability to embark on a new beginning. They were certainly operative in my own case.

I have tried to indicate that whenever someone cannot move on from survival mode there are likely to be complex reasons for that stasis. They are not always immediately obvious. The stronger the personality, the more capable people are of rationalization and concealment, even from themselves. It may take months, or even years, before the truth can set them free.

Freedom does not necessarily mean that a person like myself will automatically vary his or her lifestyle, nor does it mean that someone like Laura will necessarily remarry. Freedom to choose is what matters, a freedom that did not formerly exist. We are free to choose what kind of happiness or fulfilment we want to have. That is all.

Guilt

Principles and fears apart, guilt may also be a potent factor in preventing someone from being able to move on to a fresh start in life. In every human life, in every human relationship, particularly one as intimate as marriage or committed partnership, there are errors of judgement, mistakes, sins against the other or others, that bind us to guilt if we are not careful. For instance, if a marriage breaks down, if there is a serious disruption in a professional partnership or if a partner dies, the survivors may feel guilty in some respects. That guilt may transfer itself into a feeling that one ought to be punished for one's mistakes, that one does not deserve renewed happiness, that one can expiate one's guilt through remaining alive but unfulfilled. Again, a story may come to our help in understanding how guilt operates.

Julie was a widow. Her marriage to Caesar had not been an easy one at all. He had controlled every aspect of her life by treating her as someone who was too irresponsible to handle money. Of course, he did not say that bluntly. Instead he said 'kind' protective things to her like, 'Don't bother your pretty head about that, my darling; I'll handle it', and, 'If you want anything, you've only got to ask.' It wasn't easy to ask, as Julia found out to her cost. Asking for anything over and above her basic monthly housekeeping allowance led inevitably to questions, and then to a sermon about thrift, being thankful for small mercies, and the necessity of consideration for the poor of the world. Julia had resented her lack of financial independence. As soon as her youngest child was of school age, she had looked for and obtained a part-time job. She did this without reference to Caesar.

The row that ensued was terrible, but she had been adamant over her decision and, for the rest of their marriage, she concealed how much she earned and how much she enjoyed her relative freedom. Indeed, she had sometimes taunted Caesar with her independence and he had writhed under the lash of her tongue.

Julia's friends all expected her to thrive once Caesar had died. He had left her relatively well-off. She could afford to retire. She could live comfortably without working. She could spend her leisure by fulfilling her lifelong desire to travel the world.

Julia did none of this. Instead, she exchanged her part-time work for full-time work, moved to a smaller home, gave away a higher proportion of her income than her Christian church suggested, and remained firmly unattached. She looked successful. She looked happy. Her appearance was deceptive.

It was her dependence on alcohol that eventually brought Julia to her doctor. 'Of course, I can stop any time I want to,' she said indignantly, when her doctor disclosed the results of her liver function tests. 'It's just a matter of willpower, isn't it?'

'No, it's not as simple as that,' came the reply. 'We have to know why you're set on committing slow suicide. Why, despite all appearances to the contrary, you're so unhappy that you've got to punish yourself in this way?'

Julia was fortunate in her family doctor. A less wise person might have let her go on her way. In the end, after several attempts at self-

control had failed, Julia entered a programme of treatment. It was discovered that unrecognized guilt lay behind her self-destructive behaviour. Therapy was successful and Julia eventually emerged from her plateau existence to do what she had always wanted, but never felt able to do. She embarked on a worldwide exploration. After that, she married someone who also enjoyed travel, and they continued to enjoy the rest of their lives together.

Guilt of the kind that Julie displayed may be relatively easy to unravel, but in most of us it is more insidious. It teaches us to be content with what we already have when perhaps we ought not to stop looking for what we might achieve, given the courage to take a risk. John's case study illustrates this.

John was a homosexual. When he was a young man he had not really been aware of this, and he had married and produced four children. His first love affair with a fellow priest, who was also a close friend and colleague, was traumatic and guilt-producing. When it was over, he repented and made himself promise not to repeat the behaviour. He did not tell his wife what had happened. The sheer delight he had experienced in sexual intimacy had, however, destroyed his illusion that sexual intercourse within marriage was 'good enough'. His desire for intimacy with his wife faded. He rarely found himself able to achieve full intercourse except when the family was on their annual holiday. His wife initially ascribed their marital difficulties to his being tired out by his work, but later she began to realize that John did not love her in any way that was satisfying to her. She grew resentful of her situation and began to look elsewhere for friendship and happiness.

John had tried to convince himself that there was sufficient sexual intimacy between himself and Janice. When he realized that it was not like that for Janice he became increasingly distressed and even more impotent than he had been previously. He did not want to lose his wife, but he knew that he was sexually disabled as far as she was concerned. One day, the strain having become intolerable, he told Janice the truth about himself. Far from being upset, Janice felt happy to be trusted with this information. It made the relationship between them understandable from her point of view.

'Could we be friends?' she said. 'I don't mind about the sex, but I like your companionship. I still believe the children need two parents and I don't want to divorce you.'

In this instance, Janice and John used their freedom to stay together in a new and undemanding relationship of mutual respect and companionship. The unburdening of John's guilty secret uncovered a degree of affection for each other that they had not known existed. Staying together worked for them. It might not have done so for another couple. Another couple might have decided to go their separate ways. That, too, could be the best choice for them and for their children. Each circumstance is different.

Moral choices based simply on absolutist principles seldom work unless there is an ability to put principle ahead of every other consideration. They cannot work unless the person holding them also has the ability to carry them out. That kind of ability is not present in all people. The Roman Catholic priest who takes vows of perpetual celibacy may want to adhere to them in principle. At the time when he makes such a commitment he may think he can withstand temptation. Later, he may find out that he has not been given the gift of perpetual continence. He then has to decide whether to 'live a lie', or to stop being a priest and marry. Homosexual priests, who do not want to marry anyway, may, and often do, attach themselves to same-sex partners without such guilt. If the point of celibacy is to free a person from close personal ties, then these homosexual priests, who have liaisons with other people of the same sex, are pretending to have a freedom for service that they do not in fact possess. They are still having to live a lie. The distortions caused by concealment are sometimes worse than the admission of the truth.

Getting used to the 'status quo'

Having already described what I consider to be the major factors that impede growth in personal development, namely paradigm shifts in social attitudes, irrational fears, and guilt, I still find that there are less important factors which sometimes operate quite strongly.

Most of us, faced with disasters such as redundancy, loss of status and income, divorce, bereavement and natural disasters of all kinds can, and do, adjust to the new situation. We rejig our lifestyle and settle for less than we originally had in the way of happiness, but we do settle. In the end, we may find ourselves preferring life on the plateau to a life of onward struggle. We find it too much effort to contemplate 'moving on'. We may be afraid of failure if we take the risk of moving from familiar territory into an unknown future.

Certainly this fear of taking a risk operated strongly in my own case, in respect of being able to accept a shift from being a deacon in the Church in Wales to becoming a priest. I return, then, to my own story, which will serve to illustrate the pleasantness of the plateau and also begin to explain why and how some people do move off it.

When the Church in Wales decided not to ordain women to the priesthood, I continued to campaign for a change in its attitudes and laws. I was very clear in my own mind that women priests would bring benefits to the church. I was also convinced that priesthood would come to women younger than myself, but not to me personally. I thought that I must settle for being a permanent deacon. Over the next three years, I worked hard at this as a kind of personal calling, seeing it as a way out of the disappointment, a way that was compatible with my strong Christian beliefs. I succeeded. So when, some three years later, on 18 September 1996, the Church in Wales Governing Body lifted the restrictions and said that women could now become priests, I did not want to offer myself for scrutiny as to whether or not this was a true vocation for me.

I was well aware that I was afraid of making the change because I did not want to face renewed hostility of any kind. The people in my parish had largely settled down to accepting me as a deacon. Some of them, I knew, would not be able to accept me as a priest. Was it not better to stay a deacon and preserve the 'status quo', and avoid hostility at my time of life? I knew that I had already had a breakdown in health once in my lifetime, when I could no longer cope with overt hostility. I did not want to risk that happening again, particularly as I was now a widow without the support of a beloved husband. I had already made life vows as a solitary person living in the style of a nun and I did not want to disturb that very settled way of life. Consequently, I set my mind against ordination for myself. At the time, I was unaware of a punitive tendency in my nature that was also operative in my desire to remain a deacon.

I had, I suppose, reckoned without the Holy Spirit. From 18 September 1996 until 11 January 1997, when the first women deacons were ordained to the priesthood of the Church in Wales, conflict raged inside me. My general health deteriorated. My emotional health took a nosedive. I began to hope that I would die before I had to make the decision. My spiritual health declined as well, so that I longed for other people to make the decision for me. I could not avoid decision-making so easily, however. I remained alive.

I remained well enough physically and mentally to be able to proceed with ordination should I wish to. No one else would make the decision for me. Our diocesan bishop simply assumed that all the women deacons in the diocese who believed themselves called to priesthood were indeed called to that office in the Church, and he proposed to ordain us all unless we ourselves declined.

The arguments for and against becoming a priest were evenly divided. I did not know what to do. What tilted the balance in my case, as it so often had done before, was my inherited fear of being a coward. My father had often confessed to me that he was mortally afraid every time he undertook the tasks of an undercover intelligence agent.

He would not, however, allow fear to prevent him from doing what he thought to be right. I was a 'chip off the block': fear could not be allowed to dominate my life. I had to do what I believed to be right, whatever the cost. The call to priesthood remained strong, even though I knew I could never hold any responsibility in the Church in Wales because I was already past retiring age. So I decided to take the risk and to move on.

In my own mind I have likened taking this decision to that of leaving a plateau of safety in order to reach a goal. It was like taking the calculated risks involved in climbing a mountain. I believed God had called me to priesthood. Fear stood in the way. Therefore fear had to be overcome. There is no more merit in deciding to climb the mountain of fear than there is in deciding that one cannot go on with a physical climb because the risks are too great. Staying on the plateau is not necessarily a failure. It, and a subsequent descent into the valley, might be the right decision, as many physical mountaineers and geographical explorers have found. It is, I suppose, a matter of temperament. That temperament is partly forged by one's genes, partly by previous experiences of challenges in life, partly by one's own value system. What seems to me to be important is the willingness to make a decision and to stick by it.

So what are the precise factors that help someone like me to move? If we again return to the story of St Paul's journeys in Acts, we might think that he had no choice in the matter of leaving Malta. He was a prisoner under guard. Certainly, by that time he had no choice, but his being there in Malta was the result of many choices that he had made after he had become a Christian, an itinerant preacher, a self-supporting teacher and a healer of people's lives. Had he made other choices he would not have come to be shipwrecked off Malta at all. It is the same for all of us. We arrive at certain points in our lives because of the choices we have made previously. What interests me is why some people are content simply to survive, while others, like me need to move on.

7

Moving on to new beginnings

'Three months later we set sail on a ship that had
wintered at the island.'
(Acts 28:11a)

In mixing my metaphors between allusions to ships and mountains, I
may have tested my readers' patience. Nevertheless, both images have
been important in my own life, which I see as one long journey,
sometimes in the relative safety of a large ship, at other times clinging
to a ledge halfway up a mountain. The most exciting times of my life
have been when the ship has gone down at sea or when I have moved
from the safety of my ledge to meet fear head on. Such adventures
may not appear to be of my own making but, as with most survivors
of repetitive disasters, I find that periods of plateau existence after
initial survival are often followed by a renewed determination to
move on. Using my own life as a prime reference point, but also
taking into consideration the lives of people I have known and
admired, I have asked myself what are the principal factors that have
enabled me and others to move off the plateau of survival towards a
new beginning, a fresh start, another adventure?

The joy of risk

Initially, I had labelled this section as *joie de vivre*, the joy of life. I think
that, on the whole, it is difficult for people to take risks unless they are
happy to be alive and also reasonably full of energy. Plateau existence
is often the only option for people who have decided to remain alive,
in the literal sense of that word, but who cannot face the possibility of
losing what they have gained for the sake of what they might gain. In
my case, however, I took a risk when I was not at all well, when I was

positively unhappy and when the grass on the other side of the divide did not look at all green. As I have already indicated, a major factor in my taking this risk was a genetic predisposition to overcoming fear simply because, like my father, I could not face being a coward. A lesser fear was conquered by a greater one. That may seem rather a negative reason for making an important decision. I would prefer to say that I was imbued with a desire to serve God, a conviction that I was called to priesthood and needed to be willing to take risks for God's sake. I know, however, that this is not the full truth. My movement towards priesthood started from a more human level.

Taking risks, however, was also part of my personality. Both my parents took risks with their own lives when they were intelligence agents in Russia during and after the First World War. They survived. Other agents did not. Maybe the excitement of taking risks was in their blood and, therefore, in mine. I think, however, there was more to it than that. I think the excitement of risk was an acquired one as well as an inherited one. I took risks all through my working life because of the excitement of gambling between failure and success.

Certainly my own risk-taking has never been calculated. It has been spontaneous, impetuous, even foolhardy. I took a risk in leaving my intended career as a medical practitioner for one as a nun–doctor. That took me to Africa where I also took risks in my surgical work. When things went wrong and I found myself in hot water, I was rescued by my future husband. He and I took major risks in getting married when our ages, cultures and previous experiences were so disparate. That decision paid off. Others did not.

We took a chance when we returned to Africa after we had our first child, and that venture failed. I made a calculated decision when I moved from a good stable job as a family doctor in a suburb of London to a psychiatric hospital. That did not work out at all well for either of us. So I had to return to general practice. We took a risk, mostly on my initiative, when I left family medicine to become a school doctor. After initial disaster, that was a wonderful seven years. Later on, as a widow, I gambled when I left the safety and respectability of established convent life for the solitary way. That has not turned out as I expected it would, but I cannot say it has been a failure from my point of view. I continue to take small risks every day of my life. Staying on the plateau leads me to boredom and ultimately to depression. Taking risks is more exciting, especially when they come off.

When I look around at what other people do and do not do, I find some people who stay at home and build up the stability of the community. They may take small risks, but, on the whole, they are content with stability and personal security. Then there are others who venture out of the safety of the community to pioneer unknown territory. When that territory is gained, other people may settle there while the outriders, so to speak, tend to move on. Happiness comes from knowing which kind of person you are and not trying to become like the other.

So, the fear of being a coward and the joy of taking risks prompted me forwards when other people might have remained stable and secure. I can trace that dyad in the lives of some explorers, mountaineers and politicians, as well as in my own life. One of the heroes of my younger life was a poet and a skilled mountaineer, Wilfred Noyce. He it was who established the base on the South Col of Everest from which Tenzing and Hillary made the successful first ascent of Mount Everest in 1953. I knew him long before that successful expedition: as a teenager I used to sit and talk with him about Dante's great poems and we discovered this mutual impulse towards the overcoming of fear and the joy of risk-taking. Noyce loved life. He also loved adventure. He eventually lost his life on another high-mountain expedition. When I heard of his death, I could not be sorry for him. He had died doing what he wanted to do. I was, of course, sorry for his wife and children, whom I did not know. My own life was shaped by admiration for pioneers such as Noyce, and it still is.

The joy of freedom

When I trace the reasons why I made the decision to move from convent life to the solitary way, and from being a deacon to being a priest, I can see that the joy of freedom had much to contribute to my eventual choice. I had found great freedom within the limitations of monastic obedience and I positively enjoyed being a deaconess and then a deacon. So why move? Why take such risks? The answer lies in a desire for the freedom to exercise personal responsibility and authority.

Many people think of freedom as a state in which a person is able to do what he or she likes to do. In certain circumstances that is true. For a limited time people on holiday, for instance, are free from all their usual daily responsibilities. It is also true that freedom from poverty allows people to exercise a greater freedom in respect of their choices about where they can afford to live and what they can afford to buy. Having enough money enables people to move from living at bare subsistence level to living with some ability to make choices. Those who are released from prison or a hostage state are subsequently free to determine where they go and what they will do each day. It is delightful to recover from an illness and to find you are free from the limitations and restrictions that such an illness imposed.

Those kinds of freedom are precious. I had experienced the freedom of holidays, freedom from poverty and, occasionally at least, the freedom of good health, and I valued them all. It was not, however, those kinds of freedom that I wanted when I decided to become a priest rather than a deacon. It was the freedom to accept responsibility.

I had known that kind of freedom during my first twenty-eight years as a medical practitioner. During those years, I had been able to put my medical knowledge at the service of patients. I was able to share that knowledge with them and offer them appropriate advice that would help them to make informed choices. I could prescribe and refer patients to consultants when I wanted to. My training and acquired skills gave me considerable freedom, and I used that freedom responsibly. I enjoyed that responsibility.

When I became a school doctor for the last seven years of my working life in medicine, I lost the freedom to prescribe. I became unable to refer patients to anyone other than their own family doctor. I still, though, had some major responsibilities in respect of diagnosis, advice and the education of disabled children and young people.

This freedom to be a responsible person, in so far as my profession as a doctor was concerned, shielded me initially from some of the freedoms I did not have as a woman in society and in the church. I have already described the shock I received when I found that, as a married woman, I could not be responsible for my debts but had to rely on my husband's guarantee on hire-purchase agreements. From the time I became an Anglican deaconess in 1970 until the time I stopped being a medical practitioner in 1988, I had no freedom to exercise responsibility in the Church of England. I managed the extraordinary difference between my life as a doctor and my life as a deaconess by a mixture of humour and anger at the predicaments I found myself in. I was, however, protected from the full effects of that lack of freedom to exercise responsibility, by my medical and political work in society.

In 1988 I stopped being a doctor and became a deacon in the Church in Wales. I found I no longer had any authority to exercise responsible freedom. New initiatives and new work were subject to the vicar's assent. I had no authority to give God's blessing to those who needed that assurance, to absolve from sin, to preside at a Eucharist. I could not conduct weddings, though some deacons in other places could. I could conduct baptisms in the absence of the vicar and I could take funerals providing that both he and the bereaved relatives consented. Moreover, as a junior nun, I was subject to the common Rule of our order and I had virtually no freedom to exercise personal choice.

Had I never enjoyed the freedom of responsibility I might have managed better than I did. As it was, I rebelled initially and then submitted in the worst possible way by making an idol out of prompt, unthinking and often irresponsible obedience, both in my church-related work and in the convent. I suppose that was the way by which I survived. Certainly I was not all that unhappy with my infantile compliance. I did not, however, grow as a person.

Even when I reclaimed some freedom by leaving the convent, I remained handicapped. I had become accustomed to not making responsible decisions. It took time for me to vary my monastic pattern of life, to make a new pattern that was more in tune with my altered circumstances. It took time for me to realize that there was no one standing at my side to tell me what to do, what not to do. It took time to listen to the whispers of the Holy Spirit that allowed me to reclaim my freedom to overcome fear, to take risks, to live with responsible personal decisions. Such is the effect of the restriction of personal responsibility imposed by being a prisoner of ill health, a prisoner of society and even a prisoner of a voluntary decision to live subject to the authority of religious superiors and authority figures in the church. It took me a long while to reclaim that freedom, once I had lost it. It took even longer to find the nerve to ask to do what I wanted to do.

Becoming a priest would not restore me to the full exercise of responsibility. It could not, for by the time it was possible for women to be ordained in my church, I was over retirement age, could never take responsibility for a parish and could never know the delight in exercising 'a cure of souls' as a shared exercise with a diocesan bishop. As I thought about the possibilities, however, I realized that I would regain a limited amount of freedom in respect of responsibility were I to become a priest in the Church in Wales. I would be able to give God's blessing to those who wanted it. I would be able to offer people the assurance of God's forgiveness in a way that had not been officially possible to a deacon. I would be able to preside at a Eucharist. There would be times when I could substitute for an overworked vicar in taking services.

So, eventually, the joy of taking risks, together with a strong desire for the kind of freedom that would come with responsibility, enabled me to accept a new beginning. Naturally, I took account of all the bad consequences that might result from that decision. I anticipated some of them. I failed utterly to think of others – which was just as well, as I might not have gone ahead had I known about those. I did not, for instance, anticipate the strength of my own social and religious conditioning. For the whole of the first year after ordination to the priesthood, I simply did not feel that I was a priest. Like some of the congregation whom I served, and who made their views clear by refusing to receive any priestly ministry from me, I did not feel that any of my actions were valid. So I had to ignore my feelings and simply trust that the Church in Wales and my diocesan bishop were right in what they had done.

I cannot now remember when the change happened, when I began to feel I was a priest, for it was a gradual process. I do know that the people in our Christian community who mistrusted my validity eventually helped me to see that God could act through me if God wanted to. God could do anything; literally anything. If the Church in Wales had got it wrong and I was not a priest, then God could act quite independently. God could give the people who wanted it blessing, forgiveness and the grace of Holy Communion irrespective of my part in that action. I can recall laughing to myself one day when I fully accepted this. Suddenly I felt quite free. I, God's servant, mattered not at all; it was God who gave the gifts to the people of God. From that moment onwards I was completely trustful of God, and that worked its own miracle in God's own way and in God's own time.

I did not anticipate that some people who accepted the ordination of women with their minds would have so much difficulty in their hearts. Although these people were supportive theologically, they could not maintain that support when any opposition was vociferous. For a long time, much longer than my first year as a priest, when *they* wobbled, *I* wobbled. When they distrusted my work as a priest, I distrusted myself too. When they were afraid of what people might do and say, were I to take a major service of Holy Communion on one of the important festivals of the church's year like Christmas or Easter, I became equally afraid, even saying that I did not want to take such a service. When arrangements were made to let people know who was celebrating at each service I consented. This enabled people who wanted to do so, to stay away when I was presiding. I did not like the practice. The emphasis felt wrong. People should come to church to meet God, not worry about who was God's agent. Eventually, friends' protests about this, rather than my own, made it possible to alter some of the prohibitions. Now, years after these events, I am not as badly affected by other people's opinions as I once was. My trust has rooted itself in God, God who can act through anyone God chooses to, however inadequate or peculiar that person may seem to other people.

I am glad I did accept the added responsibility of priesthood. Was that all there was to it then – taking risks, enjoying the freedom of responsibility? No, of course not, but I would be dishonest if I left these two motivations out. Idealists, especially those with religious faith, should not hide their human motives behind their ideals. Nevertheless, perhaps my strongest motivations for coming off the plateau of 'good enough' survival were love and religious faith, and it is to these that I now turn.

Love

I have put love first because it is universal in a way that religious faith is not. Anyone who has fallen in love after a long period of aloneness knows the strength of that emotion in bringing about change. In my professional life I have often heard a widow or widower say, 'I'll never marry again'. Later, I have been able to share their delight when they shyly tell me that they have fallen in love and are going to marry again. I have sat with people whose self-confidence has been wrecked by a cruel divorce. I have seen that self-confidence and self-esteem boosted by a new friendship, new working companions, new intimacy.

When disaster strikes, many of us feel that we will never be the same again – and that is true: we never will be. We can, however, still move on, still become the people we are meant to be. It takes a lot of courage to allow oneself to fall in love with life again, to accept that one is lovable and that life can have a purpose.

Love, on the plateau, is different from duty, dependency and friendship in the valley of despair, when all that can be done is to survive. There are, of course, elements of love and faith present in those who do choose to survive disaster, but they are seldom perceptible to a victim whose life is in ruins. Love, on the plateau between simple survival and renewed enjoyment of life, is not only perceptible, it can also be overwhelming.

For most people, the word 'love' implies a relationship with another person, but that is not always so for people who are moving towards greater fulfilment. Take, for instance, Joanna.

Joanna was widowed when she was only thirty years old. There were no children of the marriage. Joe's death was not only catastrophic; it was horrific. He died of secondary bone cancer from a primary in a testicle. For some reason, which even his excellent doctors could not understand, Joe's pain was uncontrollable. When he died, Joanna was relieved despite her anguish. That feeling did not last. She went into a deep depression and was even suicidal at one time, soon after Joe's death. She survived and eventually returned to her work as a personal secretary to a consultant physician.

Five years after Joe's death, Joanna looked well, behaved impeccably at work and enjoyed a modest social life. Her friends felt she was well on the way to recovery. Joanna, however, knew that she had got stuck on a plateau. She was still searching for a way off that ledge. She tried a dating agency. She tried a 'singles' holiday. She thought about changing her job, even though she enjoyed it. Although she was not afraid, she did not mind taking the risks involved in finding a new partner. Yet, though she wanted to make a move away from the plateau, she found that she was unable to find the motivation to help herself to find something new to do.

One evening Joanna was at home. As usual, she was eating her meal alone in front of the television. There was a programme on view that showed a craftsman in silver at work. Joanna had seen many programmes like this before. Later, she told me that she had no idea why this one was different. She thought it might have been the sight of filigree work. She had never seen that before. At any rate, it was love at first sight.

Love necessarily invites commitment. Joanna sensibly began by going to evening classes to learn to work with silver. Finding that she had considerable talent, she took a risk, gave up her work and used a small inheritance from an aunt to take a full-time course. In time, she became a professional and earned her own living in that way. She never married, never became famous, never made a large sum of money, but she had gained far more than the satisfaction of success. She felt fulfilled in a way she had never done before.

Love is such a strong and propelling force that it can accomplish miracles in a person's life. Time and again I have seen the way in which parents' love for their children motivates them to change their lifestyle. Parents will redeploy their skills, accept hardship, even give up cherished work to care for a handicapped member of their family. Time and again I have seen children's love for their parents prompt them to heroic self-sacrifice. The same applies to any deep relationship, be it with other people or with a craft, a piece of work or a vocation. Love, of the kind I am describing, moves mountains. It can also be frightening.

Love is not a weak force. You only have to read St Paul's homily on love in his first letter to the Christians in Corinth (1 Corinthians 13) to see the strength required to persevere, to endure, to hope and to believe all things. Those who love are well motivated to endure hardships, overcome obstacles and resist antagonism in the pursuit of their goals.

I learnt about this practical, persevering love mostly at the hands of the non-Christians with whom I worked during the political campaign to secure the passing of the 1975 Sex Discrimination and Equal Opportunities Acts. Many of us had husbands and children. Many of us worked for a living. We were articulate, determined, even fierce in our pursuit of justice for women in general. We learnt our way around the political system of the country. We used our knowledge well. This meant developing unusual stamina, the strength to complete a working day and then start again, for we often worked on proposals for legislation late into each night. It meant getting petitions together, talking to friendly, and sometimes unfriendly, members of parliament. We taught ourselves to bargain effectively. We discovered how to survive disappointment and rejection. We had to take to the streets from time to time to hold protest demonstrations at the plight of less-advantaged women. We had to go on campaigning year after year. We spent time encouraging one another, so that we could prevent ourselves from absorbing the unjust epithets that were often hurled at us by opponents. Love even demanded the acceptance of unpleasant accusations by people who had never taken the trouble to find out that the women they thought of as bra-burning Amazonian warriors were, in fact, quite ordinary people who had to steel themselves to make their protests. Our daughters and grand-daughters owe such women – there were many others in all kinds of different organizations from our own – a great deal, just as we older women owe a great deal to the suffragists of earlier times. The love of a few people can bring about extraordinary changes in society, despite reactionary forces which try to preserve the status quo.

In the course of my life, I have often had to ask myself what part God's love plays in the economy of society? Certainly it is true that God's love for creation enters into and inspires a response from the whole of creation. Human beings, in particular, being conscious beings, are able to express that love. For a person of religious faith, such as myself, the ability to show human love comes from God. That human love may also be directed back to God. In my own life, the realization that I and others are objects of God's love prompts a response in me of love for God. That is expressed in love and concern for people in society. Yet the language by which I try to express this mystery is sometimes so convoluted that it obscures rather than reveals truth. By trying to unpack the mystery I may merely destroy its power in my life. Nevertheless, since it has been one of the strongest impulses in my life, I feel I must try to talk about falling in love with God as a motivating force for a change of personal direction.

I fell in love with God when I was fourteen. I did not know it at the time. My love grew tepid, as adolescent love often does. It was renewed when I was eighteen years old and, despite repeated infidelities, it has continued to be a motivating force behind every change of direction, every attempt to change attitudes in church and society, every loving relationship with my family, every friendship and every piece of work undertaken in God's name.

If you asked me, as I have often asked myself, to describe who it was that I had fallen in love with, I could not, and cannot, give you an answer. I cannot capture God unless I turn that word into an image that I myself have created. God is completely unknowable, as far as I am concerned and, despite being taught that Jesus is the human face of God, I have only a very hazy impression of the man behind the Bible narratives. What I do have, and have always related to, is Jesus' teaching as interpreted by the New Testament authors. Certain of

Christ's teachings have crystallized themselves into a code of behaviour by which I try to live.

This code of behaviour is, as I well know, one that I have selectively chosen. I would, of course, say that the impulse to choose comes from God, so there is a sense in which I believe that God inspires me to make wise choices for myself. Other people would choose differently, according to their unique temperaments, but their chosen paths might lead them in the same direction. My ideals embody the notion I have of what it means to be fully human and, because I want to become a whole person, I walk this narrow path, this way of particular moral choices in order to gain that prize.

I was brought up by my mother to respect and care for other people. I soon found that I could not do that unless I had a strong reason to behave in this way. Christ's teachings, particularly those in the Sermon on the Mount (Matthew 5–7) provided me with that motivation. Habitual respect and care (some might say compassion, but I would not go so far as that – not, at any rate, when I was a young doctor) turned into love for the unlovely, the outcast, the oppressed. These were the people that brought out the best in me. For many years I served them as a medical doctor. I enjoyed the work and I went out of my way to help where I could. Whenever I realized that human help had come to its natural end, I could still stand alongside patients as they continued on their journeys.

However, it took many more years of living before I could acknowledge that I worked not only for love of them but for love of myself. I had been conditioned as a child not to love myself; to put God first, others second and self last. It took some time and effort to overcome this way of thinking and look at things the other way round. I was helped in my task by St Bernard, a twelfth-century monk who was a practical man and a politician.

St Bernard[1], wrote a wonderful treatise on the love of God in which he describes the four stages of such love that operate in people's lives. In this treatise he points out that love is a natural affection, one of four, the others being fear, joy and sorrow.

The *first degree of love*, according to St Bernard, is to love oneself for the sake of oneself. Those who know what they want for themselves will either grab what they can and hold on to it or they will treat other people as they want to be treated themselves. Thus, if you love yourself and recognize that you need respect, care and consideration, you are more likely to be able to give respect, care and consideration to other people. If you deny those needs in yourself, you are likely at some stage in your life to deny them to others. St Bernard says that you cannot love either yourself or others unless God is at the root of that love. Loving God and following the teachings of Jesus are the ways by which we learn to love ourselves and our neighbour as ourselves (Matthew 22:39; Mark 12:31).

The *second degree of love* is love of God for what he gives to us. Human beings soon find out that they are selfish, territorial, greedy, possessive, prone to sin, positively hateful to other people if left to their own natural instincts. Many do not like being like that. They turn outside themselves for help and often, as I discovered when I was nineteen and did not like myself at all, they find help from God or from a set of ideals that inspires them to live more humanly than they could do if reliant on their own resources. It was because I could not cope with myself that I returned to God when I was a young adult. In God, and through the church that constantly reminded me of Christ's teaching, I found the kind of help I needed to live a more human life; a life in which I could begin to love both my neighbour and myself.

The *third degree of love* is love of God for what God is. There comes a point in a human life where one moves from loving Christ's teaching to loving the person who gave that teaching. It is as if, through the teaching, one comes to understand and appreciate the person behind it. Although I have already said that my impression of the man behind the teaching of the New Testament is very hazy, I do have some ideas about him. As time has gone on, I have got to know him better and, through him, I have come to know a little bit about God. Christ, and God who created him, and the Holy Spirit who is our 'Go-between God'[2]; are so mysterious that we long to know them better. We are drawn to pursue them in order to know them better. We never come to the end of that pursuit but, when we begin to follow Christ's teachings, we are irresistibly drawn into the search for the person behind that teaching. When we glimpse that person, and when, at times, we meet that presence through prayer and the sacraments, we begin to experience an exchange of love, a flowing of love from God to us and from us to God. That experience is like the experience of being in love with another person, but since God's love for us is unconditional it remains a mystery beyond expression. It is that passage of God's unconditional love towards us that helps us to begin to love God unconditionally, so that whatever we experience at

God's hands by way of personal disaster and apparent betrayal does not, in fact, diminish our love and trust in God.

This is a mystery that I have seen time and time again in my work as a doctor. Parents have not only survived the tragic death of a child, they have subsequently been able to love God more deeply and to work on behalf of other bereaved parents. A Christian friend of mine survived a particularly acrimonious divorce and, when she had recovered sufficiently, she went on to work with divorcees – to their great benefit as well as to her own. Parents of children injured at birth may rage at God initially, but I have seen them devote their lives to the love and care of those children to a degree that is heroic.

Perhaps one of the best accounts of how a person can move from resentment to acceptance of a terrible situation comes from the writings of Joni Eareckson Tada. When she was seventeen years old, Joni dived into shallow water and broke her neck. She regained consciousness to find herself on a ventilator and totally paralysed from the neck down. She wrote about the way in which she moved from self-pity to self-love for God's sake in her three autobiographical books.[3] They are worth reading and rereading whenever we are tempted to think that 'love of God for what God is' is impossible. It is not, provided that we get rid of our anthropomorphic ideas about God. These projections of our minds trap us into thinking about God as someone who positively enjoys bringing about disasters and seeing us drown in our resentment at our ill fortune. Such ideas have to go, before we can relate to God more fully.

The *fourth degree of love* of God is the love of self only for God's sake. St Bernard says that this kind of love is only attained when the person is so closely united to God that he or she is wholly 'at one' with God, so closely united that it seems as if the soul is 'a small drop of water, mingled in much wine'. The water takes on the taste and colour of the wine 'so completely that it appears no longer to exist apart from it'.[4] This allusion reminds St Bernard's readers of the custom of mixing a little water with wine at the offertory of the Eucharist. The wine represents Christ's divinity, the water his humanity. Christ's humanity and divinity are indistinguishable, yet they are separate aspects of his personhood. St Bernard envisages that our humanity will one day be taken up into Christ's divinity and so be transformed into the likeness of his resurrection body, yet we shall remain our unique selves.

St Bernard says that few people ever attain this degree of love in their lifetimes, although he conjectures that some of the martyrs must have loved God so much that they were granted this gift of supreme love by God at the time of their death. For the rest of us, he postpones such union of love until the Day of Resurrection, when, as he says, we will, 'no longer love ourselves save for his sake, and He Himself becomes His lover's Recompense, Reward eternal of eternal love'.[5] St Bernard's concept of the fourth degree of love is not easy to grasp but, occasionally, I think I begin to understand what he is talking about. Or maybe I just enjoy the prose poetry of his discourse!

I have written at some length about love as a strong motivating force at this stage in the journey from disaster towards growth into wholeness. Moving off the plateau of plain survival means finding enough courage to take risks. It involves some struggle against fear. There has to be some desire to take responsibility for one's actions, even if those actions are first inspired by God. Above all, if one is to move off the plateau, and certainly if one is to move forwards or upwards, there has to be a good amount of love present, both for oneself and others.

Faith

Just as faith was a bridge between the internal factors that help people to survive and the external factors that contribute to that ability to say 'yes' to life, so faith is a bridge between plateau, or 'good enough', existence and a renewed zest for life.

In my own life there has been a difference between survival and moving forwards to grasp the opportunity of a fuller experience of life itself. The faith that has helped me to survive personal disaster has not been the same as the religious faith that has moved me off the plateau towards renewal. For me – for others it might be different – it has been human faith that has helped me to survive, religious faith that has moved me away from the ledge where I have got stuck.

My religious faith has always included a large element of doubt: doubt in myself, doubt in the very existence of God, doubt that I am lovable enough for God to want to help me out of the abyss of despair into which I sometimes fall without any warning. Doubt, however, has strengthened my religious faith. Having a concept of a God who is outside myself, as well as within, has helped me to accept the concept of grace. Grace is a religious term used by Christians to describe help that comes to people directly from God. It sometimes may be possible to haul oneself out of a disastrous situation by one's own effort. One's own effort is, however, not always enough. Faith that there is another kind of help available, help from a supreme being called God, brings about a different kind of result. I can best describe it by referring to my husband's experience of life in Liberia during the Second World War.

Leo had spent the three years from June 1939 to June 1942 building a large church in the centre of a jungle-clearing in the hinterland of Liberia. All the materials for constructing this building had to been carried into the Mission on the backs or heads of men, who had to walk for eight hours from Buyedu, the last town in Sierra Leone, to Bolahun, the Christian town in the jungle. Each of the thirty-six iron pillars, twelve feet long and weighing over three hundred pounds, designed to support the roof of the church, had to be carried by twelve men working in relays of six at a time. In a book he wrote for our children[6] when he was already an old man, Leo commented:

> Carrying in the iron pillars and the huge wooden timbers for the roof could be likened to juggernauts on modern roads. The men jogged along with them on their heads, shouting all the time for others on the narrow road to get out of the way. How they managed on some of the winding trails is still a mystery to me. This almost miraculous feat of human endurance and strength, to say nothing of ingenuity and foresightedness really took place.[7]

Having lived in Liberia myself, and spoken to some of the porters who accomplished that task, I know that these feats were accomplished by people who had faith in God. They do not believe they could have accomplished such feats in their own strength. Each was convinced he had been given divine help to build that large church which, at that time, was the only one in the hinterland of Liberia.

By contrast, another of his experiences could have been the result of human effort alone. Early in 1942, my husband went home to America on furlough. The war made it difficult for him to get passage back to Liberia and he had to do the journey in steps, first from New York to Cape Town on a small freighter, and then from Cape Town to Freetown in Sierra Leone on an even smaller Dutch freighter. Leo again takes up the story:

> On the evening of April 4th, 1942, it being Easter Eve, we were expecting to reach Freetown on the next day. As we were sitting down

for our evening meal there was a loud bang which shook the entire ship. We had been torpedoed. Those in the stern had been killed by the missile. By the time we got up on deck the ship was beginning to sink. But there was no panic and we were able to get into four life boats before the boat finally sunk. The submarine soon surfaced and fortunately for us we were not gunned to death as many of the crew had expected. The captain of the submarine told our captain just where we were, about a hundred miles off the coast of the French Ivory Coast which was then in Vichy hands ... The four boats were able to stay lashed together. Two of them had diesel engines, but one of them took over an hour to get started. The life boats had been well stocked with drinking water and dry biscuits, and they had canvas awnings as protection from the burning sun.

There were about twelve people to each life boat so we were able to lie down on the bottom of the boats during the nights. Our meals consisted of one biscuit and a cup of water three times a day. On the fourth day we sighted land.

A small motor launch came out to meet us. The man in charge told us that if we landed we would all be interned for the rest of the war. He kindly informed us that Cape Palmas, an eastern town in Liberia, was only another day's journey away. So we went on, eventually crawling ashore with the help of a joyful crowd of people who welcomed us.[8]

That experience did not need to be attributed to divine intervention, or even to divine help. It was an experience of survival after disaster. Human courage and skill had brought the shipwrecked people safely to land. What followed next, however, was an experience directly related to the religious faith of my husband and his priest companion, Fr Joe Parsell.

The two priests could have stayed in Cape Palmas. After such an experience no one would have blamed them, and there was plenty of work for them to do there. Instead, they were eager to get back to their Mission, hundreds of mile to the west. This meant a flight to Monrovia and a wait of three weeks before men to carry their equipment could walk down to the capital from Bolahun, the Mission town. When they eventually set off on the return walk, it took ten full days and nights to hack a way through the 'entangled creepers or through swamps not knowing how deep you might sink with the next step. And all the time there was an incessant chorus of bird calls, the howling of monkeys and the crashing of animals through the undergrowth.'[9]

Arriving at the Christian town of which my husband was 'chief', they settled down to visit outstations, continue their study of the local languages, and to run the hospital, as there was no doctor available. This they did with the help of one of the lay-evangelists who was a trained nurse, an untrained nun who had a good deal of common-sense experience, and several Liberian men who had been trained in medical work by former doctors.

In telling me later about these adventures, my husband was quite clear that he had needed 'grace', outside help from God, to return to Liberia and continue to do work at the hospital for which he had never been trained. He believed that his religious faith had carried him through those years. I do too.

Religious faith, or faith in any strong ethical concept, drives people to do things that are not natural to them, that call for an effort that goes beyond the ordinary impulses and ambitions of most human beings. I do not understand religious faith and I have sometimes wished that I did not have it. But I do, and I have never been able to get away from the belief that God created me, and everyone else, to do a particular task on earth that God wants done. That belief, and a continuing dialogue with the being I call God, has had a direct and profound influence on the way I have lived my life and the choices I have made. It has caused me to heed a calling that is unusual among people of my upbringing and scientific training.

I certainly would not be living the way I am living were it not for a profound and persistent religious faith that prompts me to live a life of prayer as a solitary under religious vows. I would not have become a priest of the Church in Wales. I would not have continued to work long after the normal retiring age. No, I would be a comparatively affluent retired doctor, living in my own home, enjoying a settled and leisured way of life. Left to my own devices, I would be travelling around Britain to see my children and grandchildren as often as possible. I would take frequent opportunities to travel abroad, to revisit places I love, to see places I have never seen and now never will see. I would be going to the theatre, to concerts, to the opera. While I would be enjoying my own company for the most part, I would enjoy small dinner parties and the occasional excursion to a grand party. Instead, I am doing none of the things that are congenial to me. Yet I count myself among the happiest people on earth because I feel that I am living the way that God wants me to live, and I want, if possible, to live that way for the rest of my life.

8

Homecoming

'And so we came to Rome.'
(Acts 28:14b)

My choice of the book of the Acts of the Apostles as the source of quotations for the last three chapters is not coincidental. It is my belief that one of the reasons for the attractiveness of the Bible is that it speaks of the human condition. Admittedly, it is sometimes dealing with events that have moved into past history, sometimes with stories that embody human experience, sometimes with imaginative ideas about what the future should be like. For me, however, these three strands come together in the present moment that I experience now as a living human being.

The Bible is a compilation of writings from various writers and periods of history. When I read about events in the Bible, I can sometimes see how they fashion the events that succeed them. In a similar way, I can see that what happened to me as an individual in my youth life shaped who I became as an adult and continues to shape who I will become. Just as the Bible is a complex narrative, dealing with the interactions of many different individuals, so I can see that my own life is interwoven and shaped by many other people. Some of those people are similar to me, some very different, but all have exerted an influence on my present and future life.

When I listen to the psalms in the Bible, or read some of the parables, I appreciate how they speak of the abiding quality of the human condition. Human nature does not seem to have changed all that much since Cain killed Abel, or since Joseph's brothers proved that they were jealous about their father's love for their youngest brother by trying to kill him. When they did not succeed, they got rid of him by selling him to some Ishmaelites for twenty pieces of silver

(Genesis 37:28), ten less than Judas received for betraying Jesus (Matthew 27:3). These, and other stories, speak to me of the dark side of my own personality, but they are countered by the story and teachings of Jesus, which give me hope for myself, as well as for others. The Bible provides me with villains with whom I can identify. It also gives me heroes and heroines whom I can admire, and who help me to become the whole person I want to be. With the help of the Bible I can admit that I have a shadow side as well as a light side to my personality. I am a real person; one who, with God's help, believes that it is possible to incorporate darkness and light into a unified whole.

Whenever I read about the future hopes, longings and desires for wholeness in the Bible, I see that they contain many of my own hopes and longings and desires. I need an attractive goal. It helps me to survive disaster and to keep moving on the journey of life.

One of the themes that runs through the whole of the Bible, is that of a journey. There are detailed accounts of the travels of Abraham, and also of the adventures of Moses and the Israelites, who escaped from Egypt and went in search of the promised land. Eventually they found it, only to be thrust into exile at a later period of history. These stories, whether founded on fact or not, hearten me, for they speak about some individuals who perished before they reached their goal. These same people, nevertheless, endowed the future: eventually, the people of God did manage to survive and reach their destiny. Those who died in exile made it possible for others to return home.

When I read about the three years of Jesus' itinerant ministry, and his journey through the cross of suffering and death to his glorious ascension, I am filled with hope. I trust that my own journey through the valley of humiliating failure will eventually lead to healing of body, soul and spirit. St Paul's incredible stamina during his own missionary travels gives me courage to keep going, even when the going seems hard, the failures are repeated and I find myself in one kind of a prison or another. The fact that his homecoming to Rome led to his death worries me not at all, for death is the gateway to my own destiny, to be absorbed into God's love 'as a drop of water is absorbed into wine'.[1]

I have had a privileged life. Inherited intelligence has been aided by good education. Inherited sensitivity was protected by the recognition that it was only safe to identify with other people when they could be taken into God through prayer. Blind faith has been made more precious by the occasional glimpses of God's hands. Those hands reach through the thick curtain of doubt to reassure me that I am both lovable to God and loved by God. I have encountered many disasters on my journey of life, but it is the sense of coming home, of 'reaching Rome', that gives me such an immediate sense of fulfilment as I await the next adventure into the unknown; that of death itself.

Unlike many of my contemporaries, I have been able to achieve a goal that has given me insights into the nature of God. I never would have had those insights had I died before I could become a priest in the Church in Wales. I owe so much to those of my contemporaries who died before they could see for themselves. Their journeys have overlapped with mine. Their struggles have encouraged me to go on. Their vision of the future has sustained me through many a disaster and failure. Whenever I exercise any function of priesthood, I remember them with deep thankfulness, knowing that I and others would not be priests were it not for them. They, all of them, and especially my husband, are incorporated into my life, even though they never knew that I or any other Anglican women would become the people we are.

In order to show what homecoming can feel like it is necessary to speak very personally. As I have already said, I was past retiring age when it became possible for women to become priests in the Church in Wales. I was still ill. I had been through a long period of anxious discernment about whether or not to offer for priesthood and I had taken a risk in going forward. I have admitted that I did not feel convinced that I was a priest for the first year after ordination. I had to rely on blind obedience to the Governing Body of the Church in Wales and to my ordaining diocesan bishop. Gradually, however, I was overtaken by insights about priesthood that I could not have grasped fully had I not been ordained.

The most personal and immediate result of ordination was that I recognized the Eucharist to be a 're-calling' of both a death and a birth. I do not think that I could have known this in my flesh, so to speak, without being a priest. Becoming a priest enabled me to preside at a Eucharist. Almost as soon as I started to preside, I recognized an element in the rite that I had met before during the conception and births of my four children. I saw that, from the moment of the conception of a child, the parents, both man and woman, are in the hands of a life force that cannot be controlled. Once conception has taken place, birth is inevitable, whether it results in a miscarriage, a stillbirth or a live baby. Women who approach, and then go into, labour know that there is nothing, nothing at all, that they can do to stop it. They can only feel its force within them, flow with it, and, indeed, submit to its life-bringing impetus.

In saying this, I am not excluding non-child-bearing women or men from this knowledge. They too know this truth in their flesh. It is the harder for them sometimes because there is a sense in which they feel like bystanders, though they are not. For them, birth may feel like a 'little death'. In that sense birth and death are very similar.

I felt all that during my first presidency of a Eucharist, though I could not name what was happening to me. By the third time I presided, I had identified what was happening. From the first word of the liturgy I could no more control what was happening than I could during birth or, for that matter, during the process of dying. (I have long seen death as a birth into resurrection life, and I see my role in helping people through death as that of midwife.) At every Eucharist, we are taken up into the eternal Eucharist. It is true that I was the one saying the words, but the life-giving power was coming from God who was present from the beginning, both in the people in the congregation, in myself and beyond us, yet also content to be focused in the words that signify the gracious descent of the Holy Spirit and the real presence of Christ in the consecrated elements of his Body and Blood. Being integral to that process of his coming to us, I could no more control or stop it than I could control or stop birth or death. What was going to happen was the coming of new life. There was a sacrificial death, certainly, but also a simultaneous coming of new life.

In the course of presiding at the Eucharist, I saw what I had not really seen during the fifty preceding years of hearing the Eucharist and receiving Holy Communion. I saw it as participation in birth. I saw Jesus' necessary sacrifice and death in the same terms. I saw him not so much bleeding to death – though there is, indeed, a dying, as there is in all birth – but bleeding to bring birth out of death. There is a close analogy here with the way in which women hurt and bleed to bring new life into the world.

Men may have seen this from the beginning: maybe the presidency of the Eucharist is the nearest they come to giving physical birth and that is why some of them have been so reluctant to invite women into the priesthood. As far as I'm concerned, Christ gave birth to resurrection life through his death, and both men and women can participate in that action – which is his, not ours – through the authority of the church, when they preside at the Eucharist or, indeed, as lay co-participants. We are there in the hands of God, watching Jesus doing his work on the cross and giving birth to the new life which we receive in Holy Communion. Never before have I been so clear as I am now that the Eucharist is God's work, not ours; God's response to our need. It is not for us to command him to come, but it is our privilege to invite him. And he comes; he always comes. He gives himself to us and he feeds us.

That insight has been the most important one to me during these past three-and-a-half years. There were, of course, some more practical advantages as well. I could, for instance, assure people, whom I accompanied on their journey through life, of God's forgiveness for their sins. I no longer had to send them off to 'proper' priests for the sacrament of reconciliation. I could assure people of God's blessing with confidence. I could enter into a real partnership with my colleagues.

The ordination of women makes visible to the church what has always been real but often invisible – the true partnership of men and women. It is at its most obvious when you see a man and a woman at the altar together. I can still recall the shocking delight I felt twenty-eight years ago when I first saw co-presidency of the Eucharist in the Cathedral of St John the Divine in New York, where a nun, Canon Mary Michael Simpson, was presiding at the main Eucharist of the day supported by the Dean. I am still profoundly thankful for the way God used that event to help me to see my own worth in the eyes of God. I was also given an example of the marvellous partnership that was possible between men and women, each made in the image and likeness of God. Ordination gave me the opportunity to share that visible partnership.

The most positive outcome of my being ordained as a priest has been the 'coming home' feeling it has engendered in me. For the first time in my life I feel that I am who I am meant to be. I did not benefit from this sense of assurance as soon as I was ordained. I have only just begun to rest in that feeling, now that my health has immeasurably improved compared with what it was in the months immediately before and after my ordination.

There has been one other important effect of ordination on me, namely the recognition that I am now an inheritor of a new mode of life rather than a permanent victim of life's disappointments. A particular chain that bound me to thinking of myself as a victim, 'born before her time', was broken for ever on the day that I was ordained.

When I was a young woman it was fashionable for Christian women to be victims. If they were *real* women they expected to immolate themselves in service, either through the sacrificial life of a holy nun or through giving themselves wholly to the service of their husbands and children. Many women, myself included, felt guilty if they departed from this image that Christian society projected on to them.

Victim spirituality is all too easy to acquire. According to the thought engendered by this spirituality, Jesus suffered for us on the cross. It follows that we must suffer whatever crosses are given to us. Since Jesus was endlessly forgiving, we must suffer injustice without complaint and with perpetual forgiveness. Since Jesus loved his enemies and died for them, we must love our enemies in the same way. The example of many heroic saints, their austerities, their patience under persecution and their martyrdom, was used to encourage us to emulate them. Emulate them we did, allowing people to trample on us, rejoicing that we were called to suffer with Jesus, even sometimes foolishly counting up the times we had offered our small pains in reparation for some impenitent sinner in our circle. We were, we thought, acquiring merit.

This kind of spirituality is logical. Its emphasis, however, can be on suffering for its own sake rather than on the love that enabled Jesus to endure suffering 'for the sake of the joy that was set before him' (Hebrews 12:2). Suffering that is embraced through love is very different from that which is courted for its own sake. As a young woman, I courted suffering through asceticism. Maybe I could only learn about the kind of suffering that is the consequence of love through that phase of my life. Others come to it more naturally.

Eventually, I came to understand the cross in a new way. My contemplation of Jesus on the cross gradually led me to understand that event in the light of Christ's victory in bringing resurrection life into the world. The emphasis of my life began to move away from the cross to the new life that it brought, to a sense of gratitude that I and others could claim some of the fruits of Jesus' victory.

These fruits were not immediately apparent in times of trouble; when, for instance, my mother was dying in one hospital, my husband was desperately ill in another hospital, fifteen miles away, and our children needed to be fed through my going out to work every day. All I could do in those circumstances was to numb my feelings and keep going from moment to moment. With hindsight, though, I see that it was not my victim spirituality that helped me the most. It was my belief in resurrection life. It was Love and Life that drove me on. It was the words, 'Jesus is Lord' – those words that were the catchword of the early Christians and that were invariably on their lips when they died – that sustained me through this period of difficulty in my life and through many other challenging times of hardship.

'Jesus is Lord' is a phrase that sounds rather antiquated to our modern ears because 'lordship', like 'kingship', has connotations that can lead us to think of someone who has dominion over us; someone to whom we owe fealty and who has power over our lives. I do not see it like that at all. The phrase speaks of life, for it means that Jesus has overcome sin, suffering, evil and death and enabled me to enter into the joy of that victory through living in a new mode of life; resurrection life.

Of course, I am not immune from further disasters. I know that. I know that I will die. I know that my priesthood could become non-functional at any time during the next few years, either through illness or through the advent of a new vicar who might not want me around. I know that I will not be able to go on working indefinitely. Yet the fact that I have known what it is to 'come home', to be who one was meant to be, will, I believe, stand me in good stead when those situations come along. I have met many old men and women who are imprisoned, in bed, in wheelchairs, or in the throes of painful illnesses. Some of them have achieved what they wanted to achieve in life. They are happy. I am among them.

It has taken me a very long time to see the cross as the gateway to life, and longer still for me to go through that gateway to find that new life, but now I begin to see life in a different way because I see the cross from a different viewpoint. Now, certain episodes in the New Testament, especially the Acts of the Apostles, begin to make real sense to me. When Peter spoke to the assembly gathered at Pentecost, and when he and John healed a cripple at the gate of the temple, they were aware of Jesus as their risen Lord. When Stephen was being stoned, he gazed into heaven. He saw 'the heavens opened and the Son of Man standing at the right hand of God' (Acts 7:55). Saul met Jesus on the road to Damascus and his life was turned around by that encounter. These people were not sustained in their suffering by victim spirituality. They were sustained by the vision of Jesus as lord of life, lord over death. He was their constant companion, friend, guide. He was their way, their life and their truth. That is what 'Jesus is Lord' means to me too.

The cross is real enough. I do not try to escape suffering. I do not try to lift myself into an illusory heaven so that I do not feel pain. I know that I will be engulfed by it and be afraid, but I also know that the living presence of Jesus is what sustains me through all suffering as I pass through its gateway into new life. When my time comes to die, I know that my mortal flesh will experience dissolution, but I also believe that the presence of Jesus will help me to enter into his joy.

I do not feel that my Christian beliefs separate me from other human beings. I remain a human being who has had personal experience of disaster and survival. My human belief that there is some purpose in survival, growth and making a fresh start is one that I share with many other survivors. Although I am aware that the doctrines of Christianity are not helpful to some of my fellow survivors, my own religious faith has helped me to interpret disaster and survival in a way that is profoundly meaningful to me.

The writing of this book has not been an academic exercise. It has been written in the hope that one person's experiences may resonate with those of some of my readers; that there are elements in a personal account that might help other people to survive the experience of disaster, grow through it and eventually delight in the fresh start they are able to make.

References

Chapter 2

1   Kroll, Leopold, *Life's Thoughts*, (printed privately in 1987 after his death, for his children and grandchildren), p. 4.
2   Ibid., p. 8.
3   Kroll, Una, *Forgive and Live*, London: Mowbray, 2000. Also, see notes in that book for further valuable reading on the subject of forgiveness.

Chapter 4

1   Sandford, E. G., *Frederick Temple, an Appreciation* (with biographical introduction by William Temple), London: Macmillan, 1907.
2   Ibid., p. xv.
3   Ibid., p. xv.
4   Ibid., p. xxiv.
5   These are out of print. Sadly, I have not been able to trace their publishers.

Chapter 5

1   Scott, Robert Falcon, *Scott's Last Expedition*, London: Smith Elder & Co., 1913.
2   Tiltman, Marjorie Hessell, *God's Adventurers*, London, Bombay, Sydney: Harrap, 1933, p. 45.
3   *The Times*, Monday 19 June 2000, p. 10.
4   Carter, Rita, *Mapping the Mind*, London: Weidenfeld & Nicholson, 1998, pp. 13–14.
5   *The Book of Common Prayer*, Church in Wales, p. 639.
6   Sackville-West, Victoria, *The Eagle and the Dove*, London: Michael Joseph, 1943, p. 76.
7   Donne, John, *Devotions* (2nd edn, 1953), quoted in *Oxford Dictionary of Quotations*, p. 186.
8   Schlink, Basilea, from her autobiography.

Chapter 6

1   The Bishop of Worcester, the Rt Revd Peter Selby, was excluded from a

Worcester parish in November 1999. For details see the *Church Times* reports on the controversy between the Bishop of Worcester and the Revd Charles Raven, team vicar of St John's Kidderminster, reported in December 1999, and continued until June 2000, when two retired Ugandan bishops were brought in to confirm young people against the express orders of the Bishop of Worcester, the Rt Revd Peter Selby, and the Archbishop of Canterbury, the Most Revd George Carey. See also the condensed report in *The Tablet*, 11 December 1999, p. 1695.

2   *Oxford Dictionary of the Christian Church*, ed. F. L. Cross and E. A. Livingstone, 3rd edn, Oxford: OUP, 1997, p. 1240. Also Hebblethwaite, P., *Pius VI, The First Modern Pope*, London: HarperCollins, 1993.

3   *Humanae Vitae*, published on 25 July 1968, stated that artificial contraception was wrong and that no methods of birth control other than the notoriously unsafe 'rhythm method' could be used by members of the Roman Catholic Church. This teaching has been widely disregarded by communicant members of the church ever since the publication of *Humanae Vitae*.

4   See the Report of the Meeting of the Governing Body of the Church in Wales, published after the debate during April 1994.

Chapter 7

1   St Bernard of Clairvaux (1090–1153) was a Cistercian abbot. His *Book on the Love of God* is one of two great books on the subject in Catholic literature. The other is St Francis de Sales' *Treatise on Divine Love*, written four hundred years later, in 1616.

2   See John V. Taylor's *The Go-between God, The Holy Spirit and the Christian Mission*, London: SCM Press, 1972, for a fuller exposition of this phrase.

3   Eareckson Tada, Joni, *Joni, Start of a Journey*, London: Marshall Pickering, 1980 [1991]. See also *A Step Further, Growing Closer to God through Hurt and Hardship*, London: Marshall Pickering, 1991, and *Choices, Changes, Moving Forward with God*, London: Marshall Pickering, 1991.

4   Hardon, John A. (ed.) *The Treasury of Catholic Wisdom*, New York: Doubleday, p. 199.

5   Ibid., p. 203.

6   Kroll, Leo, *Life's Thoughts*.

7   Ibid., Bk I, p. 21.

8   Ibid., Bk I, pp. 21–2.

9   Ibid., Bk I, p. 23.

Chapter 8

1   See note 4, chapter 7.